MW00636657

UNFOUND
TREASURES
OF MEXICO

Español and English

Copyright © 1995 by Charles A. Kenworthy

Library of Congress Catalog

ISBN 0-9632156-4-7
Published in the United States of America by:

Quest Publishing
P.O. Box 260100
Encino, California 91426

For information contact author and publishers at the above address.

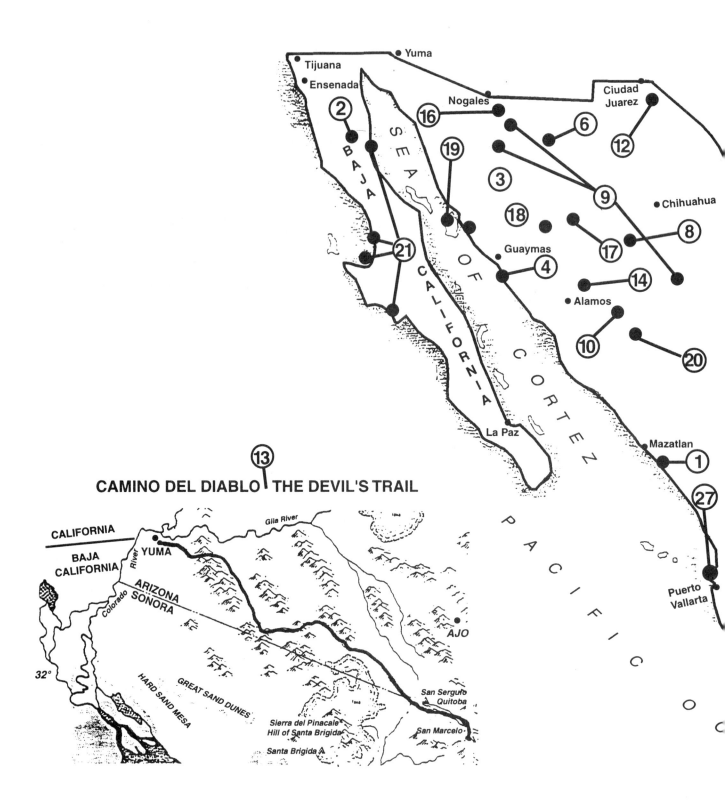

CAMINO DEL DIABLO ┃ THE DEVIL'S TRAIL

Tesoros No Encontrado
En Mexico   "Carlos"

Unfound Treasures
of Mexico

© Charles A. Kenworthy

DEDICATED TO MY LONGTIME MEXICAN, LATINO AND SPANISH AMIGOS WITH WHOM I HAVE HAD THE PLEASURE OF WORKING WITH IN THE SEARCH AND RECOVERY OF TREASURES AROUND THE WORLD. INCLUDED ARE THE ARCHIVISTS AND SUB-ARCHIVISTS OF MEXICO CITY, THE STAFF MEMBERS OF THE NATIONAL MUSEUM OF ANTHROPOLOGY AND THE SUB-ARCHIVISTS OF SPAIN'S ARCHIVES. ADDITIONALLY, I DEDICATE THIS BOOK TO THE TWO MEXICAN FAMILIES THAT BROUGHT ME THEIR LONG HELD SPANISH/MEXICAN CODED TREASURE MAPS WHICH THEY DIDN'T UNDERSTAND AND TOGETHER WE WERE SUCCESSFUL IN FINDING TWO IN ARIZONA AND ARE CURRENTLY HOT ON THE TRAIL OF ANOTHER ONE IN CALIFORNIA.

DEDICADO A MIS AMIGOS DE MUCHOS ANOS, MEJICANOS, LATINOS Y ESPAÑOLES QUE A TANIDO EL PLACER DE TRABAJAR EN BUSCA Y RECUPERACION DE TESOROS A REDONDO EL MUNDO. INCLUIDO LOS ARCHIVOS Y SUB-ARCHIVOS DE MEXICO, Y LOS MIEMBROS PERSONALES DEL MUSEO. NACIONAL DE ANTROPOLOGIA Y LOS SUB-ARCHIVOS DEL LOS ARCHIVOS DE ESPAÑA. EN ADICION QUIERO DEDICAR ESTE LIBRO A LAS DOS FAMILAS MEJICANAS QUE ME PRESTARON SU MAPAS ANTIGUS EN CODIGO DE TESORO ESPAÑOLAS/MEJICANOS. LAS FAMILAS NO ENTIENDEN LAS MAPAS, PERO JUNTOS OBTENIMOS EXITO EN DOS TESOROS EN ARIZONA, Y ANDAMOS CERCA DE OTRO TESORO EN CALIFORNIA.

Table of Contents

A BIG "THANK YOU" TO CATARINO CASTRO, LALO TRETO, JESUS ROJAS, JUAN PERALTA, MARIA AND RICARDO GONZALES WHO HAVE BEEN AND CONTINUE TO BE OF GREAT ASSISTANCE IN HELPING US FIND SOME OF THOSE POTS OF GOLD AT THE END OF RAINBOWS.

ALSO A VERY SPECIAL "THANKS" TO THE TREASURE HUNTER AND TRANSLATER OF THIS BOOK, GILBERT TRUJILLO OF APACHE JUNCTION, ARIZONA.

UN "GRAN AGRADECIMENTO" PARA CATARINO CASTRO, LALO TRETO, JESUS ROJAS, JUAN PERALTA, MARIA Y RiCARDO GONZALES POR SU AYUDA EN EL PASADO, Y POR EL PRESENTE EN DECUBRIR ESAS OLLAS DE ORO EN LOS EXTREMOS DEL ARCO IRIS.

TAMBIEN CON GRACIAS ESPECIAL PARA EL CASADOR DE TESOROS Y TRADUCRO DESTE LIBRO, GILBERTO TRUJILLO DE APACHE JUNCTION, ARIZONA.

IN ALL THE WORLD I CONSIDER **MEXICO** AS BEING SECOND **ONLY TO PERU** IN THE AREAS OF UNFOUND TREASURES AND LOST/HIDDEN MINES OF IMMEASURABLE WEALTH.

MEXICO'S IMMENSE UNFOUND TREASURES BEGIN WITH THE HIDDEN MAYAN AND AZTEC TREASURES.

NEXT CAME THE 1810 TO 1821 REVOLUTIONARY PERIOD WHEREIN FATHER MIGUEL HIDALGO GATHERED THE INDIANS, PEONS, THE ENSLAVED AND THE MEXICANS TO REVOLT AGAINST SPAIN'S RULE, AN ELEVEN-YEAR PERIOD WHERE THE MEXICANS WON THEIR INDEPENDENCE FROM SPAIN. DURING THESE ELEVEN YEARS OF FIGHTING, SPAIN WAS FORCED TO RECALL ITS SOLDIERS FROM THE NORTHERLY AREAS WHERE THEY HAD PROTECTED MANY HUNDREDS OF MINES, COMMUNITIES AND MISSIONS. THOUSANDS OF TREASURES, BOTH LARGE AND SMALL, AS WELL AS MINES, WERE HIDDEN BY MINERS, MINE OWNERS, FAMILIES, SOLDIERS AND MISSIONS WITH THE INTENTION OF RETURNING ONE DAY TO RECOVER WHAT THEY HAD HIDDEN — BUT THEY NEVER RETURNED BECAUSE SPAIN LOST AND MEXICO BECAME INDEPENDENT. THEN BETWEEN 1821 AND 1847 MEXICO HAD MANY, MANY REVOLUTIONS AND OVER 20 DIFFERENT PRESIDENTS AND GOVERNMENTS. IN 1848 MEXICO LOST ITS NORTHERNMOST LANDS TO THE UNITED STATES. THERE WAS JUST TOO MUCH CONSTANT TURMOIL TO ALLOW AN ORGANIZED AND CONCENTRATED EFFORT TO FIND THESE LOST TREASURES AND HIDDEN MINES. BY FAR THE MAJORITY ARE STILL TODAY EXACTLY WHERE THEY WERE HIDDEN AND/OR BURIED MANY YEARS AGO — UNFOUND.

WE HAVE BEEN QUITE FORTUNATE IN HAVING LOCATED TWO TREASURES IN MEXICO; HOWEVER, THESE WERE BOTH LESS THAN 80 MILES INSIDE THE BORDER. I WAS CONCERNED ABOUT GOING AFTER OTHERS BECAUSE THEY WERE DEEPER IN MEXICO AND THE GOVERNMENT'S LAWS WERE QUITE SEVERE. TODAY I UNDERSTAND THAT IT IS MUCH EASIER AND THAT THE GOVERNMENT MIGHT ISSUE TREASURE TROVE PERMITS — IF YOU APPLY.

THE VERY BEST THAT A TREASURE HUNTER/LOST MINE HUNTER CAN EVER HOPE FOR IS THAT HIS INFORMATION IS CORRECT AND ACCURATE AND THAT HIS MINE/TREASURE ACTUALLY **DID** EXIST AT ONE TIME. THEN, THE ONLY UNKNOWN FACTOR IS **DID SOMEONE ALREADY FIND IT — AND DEAL WITH IT QUIETLY??**

THE NEXT, AND ALL IMPORTANT FACTOR IS THE HUNTER'S KNOWLEDGE/UNDERSTANDING OF SIGNS, SYMBOLS, TRAIL MARK-ERS, TRAIL SIGNS AND CODES USED ON MAPS AND IN THE FIELD. TREASURE "STORY" WRITERS HAVE MISLED THE HUNTER FOR MANY MANY DECADES. ONE WRITER MUST HAVE SURELY COPIED FROM ANOTHER AND NEVER DID RESEARCH ON HIS OWN TO OUR DETRIMENT. FOR EXAMPLE: "THE HIDDEN TREASURE IS HIDDEN IN A COVERED MINE TWO LEAGUES SOUTHWEST OF 'X'". THE WRITER GOES ON TO TELL US THAT A LEAGUE WAS BETWEEN THREE AND THREE AND ONE HALF MILES IN DISTANCE. THAT IS TRUE FOR A **NAUTICAL** (OCEAN) LEAGUE BUT **NOT** ON LAND. A **STATUTE** (LAND) LEAGUE WAS **2.18 MILES**. WITHOUT QUESTION, MANY HUNTERS MUST HAVE SPENT YEARS SEARCHING **WELL BEYOND THEIR TRUE AREA** OF INTEREST — DUE TO THE STORY WRITERS.

BEGINNING IN 1974 I BEGAN MAKING CONTACT BOTH DIRECTLY AND INDIRECTLY WITH ARCHIVISTS AND SUB- ARCHIVISTS IN FRANCE, SPAIN AND THE VATICAN. MEXICO CITY'S ARCHIVES WERE COMPLETELY "OFF LIMITS", HOWEVER, "ARRANGEMENTS" WERE MADE THROUGH A MINISTER OF THE NAVY AND I DEVELOPED AN OUTSTANDING "SOURCE". BEGINNING IN 1978 I BEGAN RECEIVING NOTIFICATIONS OF "FINDINGS" FROM VARIOUS ARCHIVES. NOT HAVING SEEN THE "INFORMATION" AVAILABLE, I WOULD GUESS AT A VALUE AND MAKE AN OFFER FOR COPIES. WE HAVE RECEIVED MANY COPIES OF HIDDEN TREASURES AND MINES, BOTH IN MAP FORM AND HAND WRITTEN DOCUMENTS. UNFORTUNATELY, THE MAJORITY DO NOT SHOW OR INDICATE THE STATE, AREA OR EVEN THE COUNTRY TO WHICH THE MAPS REFER.

IN 1983 A LETTER ARRIVED STATING THAT 116 PAGES HAD BEEN FOUND RELATING TO THE KING OF SPAIN'S RULES AND REGULATIONS ON MINING AND EXPLORATION IN THE NEW WORLD. INCLUDED WERE THIRTY-FOUR PAGES OF CODED SIGNS AND SYMBOLS TO BE USED IN DOCUMENTS AND ON MAPS AND THEIR MEANINGS. ALSO INCLUDED WERE DRAWINGS OF TRAIL MARKERS AND MONUMENTS THAT SPAIN REQUIRED TO BE CONSTRUCTED, "UNDER PAIN OF SPAIN", ALONG ALL TREASURE/MINE TRAILS.

TOWARD THE END OF THE 1500'S, NEW MEXICO WAS COLONIZED BY THE SPANISH UNDER ITS FIRST GOVERNOR JUAN DE ONATE. ONATE ESTABLISHED SAN GABRIEL AS THE FIRST CAPITAL OF NEW MEXICO, BUT IT FAILED TO PROSPER. SPAIN REPLACED ONATE WITH PEDRO DE PERALTA WHO THEN ESTABLISHED SANTA FE AS THE CAPITAL. IT WAS HERE IN SANTA FE THAT THE PALACE OF GOVERNORS WAS COMPLETED IN 1609. THIS PALACE WAS TO GOVERN **NORTHERN MEXICO**. ADJOINING THE PALACE OF GOVERNORS, THE SAN MIGUEL CATHEDRAL WAS CONSTRUCTED AND IN OPERATION IN 1636.

THIS WAS THE CENTRAL POINT FOR THE CHURCH NOT ONLY IN SEEKING CONVERTS, BUT TO HELP SOLVE THE MAJOR PROBLEMS DEVELOPING IN THE PALACE OF GOVERNORS. IT SEEMS THAT THE CHRISTIANIZED MINERS REBELLED IF THEY DID NOT HAVE A FRAY/PADRE WITH THEM TO HEAR THEIR LAST CONFESSION OR GIVE THEM THE LAST RITES AT THE DISTANT MINING OPERATION (AND THERE WERE MANY DEATHS). SO, IT WORKED WELL FOR BOTH SPAIN AND THE CHURCH.

THE CHURCH WAS ABLE TO SPREAD THE WORD IN NEW AND DISTANT AREAS OF NEW MINING AND EXPLORATION BEING DONE BY SPAIN, AND THE "RELIGIOUS" MAN'S PRESENCE GAVE "CALM AND CONFIDENCE" TO THE MINING/EXPLORATION GROUPS THAT HAD BEGUN TO REBEL MORE FREQUENTLY. IN THIS MANNER OF COOPERATION, THE CHURCH AND SPAIN WORKED HAND IN HAND AND ASSISTED EACH OTHER IN THEIR SEPARATE GOALS.

THE PALACE WAS THE HEADQUARTERS OF SPAIN'S ENFORCEMENT OF THE KING'S RULES AND REGULATIONS **IN TODAY'S NORTHERN MEXICO**, CALIFORNIA, TEXAS, ARIZONA, COLORADO, UTAH, NEW MEXICO, NEVADA, LOUISIANA, KENTUCKY, ETC. THE MAJOR PART OF TODAY'S MEXICO ITSELF WAS GOVERNED OUT OF **MEXICO CITY**. MINING AND EXPLORATION ACTIVITIES WERE THE PRIMARY DUTIES OF THE PALACE: COLLECTING FROM THE HACIENDAS, MINERS AND RELIGIOUS THE KING'S 15 TO 20% AND SEEING TO TREASURE TRANSPORT BACK TO SPAIN, TEACHING EACH HACIENDA THE CODES AND SYMBOLS TO USE ON TREASURE MAPS, THE MONUMENTS AND THEIR MEANING AND HOW TO CONSTRUCT THEM TO-AND-FROM THE MINE OR HIDDEN TREASURE. THEY TAUGHT AND FURNISHED TWO WALKERS AND COMPASS/MAP-MAKERS TO EACH MINING HACIENDA. AFTER MINE ESTABLISHMENT THEY WOULD FURNISH A MINIMUM OF TWO MONUMENT MAKER SUPERVISORS TO MARK THE TRAIL. THEREAFTER, UPON THE PALACE'S RECEIPT OF THE MAPS (BOTH TREASURE AND TRAIL) IT WOULD SEND ITS OWN GROUP TO FOLLOW THE HACIENDA'S MAPS TO THE MINE SITE AND REPORT BACK TO THE PALACE ON THE PRECISION OF TRAIL MONUMENTS AND THE CODED TREASURE MAP. THEN, THE PALACE SENT COPIES OF THE MAPS TO THE KING OF SPAIN, THE PALACE IN MEXICO CITY AND RETAINED ONE IN SANTA FE. THE MAPS WERE TO INSURE THAT IF A DISASTER BEFELL THE MINERS OR THE HACIENDA, SPAIN COULD AGAIN FIND THE MINE AND THE KING WOULD NOT LOSE HIS PERCENTAGE.

THE **VATICAN (ROME) ARCHIVES** MAY WELL CONTAIN MORE RECORDS THAN SPAIN DOES OF SPAIN'S EXPLORATION AND MINING ACTIVITIES IN THE NEW WORLD FOR THE FOLLOWING REASONS: 1. SPAIN'S ARCHIVES HAD NUMEROUS DISASTERS OF FLOODS AND FIRES. 2. SPAIN'S FILES HAVE NEVER BEEN ORGANIZED, I.E.: BUNDLES OF DOCUMENTS DATED 1682 TO 1685 WILL CONTAIN LETTERS, ETC., DATED MID 1700'S. 3. THE "RELIGIOUS" APPOINTED TO THE MINING GROUPS WAS, OF COURSE, ONE OF THE HIGHER EDUCATED IN THE GROUP AND FREQUENTLY WOULD ASSIST **OR BE** THE CODED MAP-MAKER. IN

EITHER CASE, A **COPY** MIGHT EASILY FIND ITS WAY TO ROME. LITTLE, HOWEVER, WOULD HAVE COME FROM THE JESUITS WHO, DURING THOSE DAYS, KEPT MOST OF THEIR INFORMATION TO THEIR OWN "SOCIETY" (THE SOCIETY OF JESUS "S.J."), AND THEIR ARCHIVAL FILES ARE JUST ABOUT IMPOSSIBLE TO GET INTO.

MAPS ARE FULL OF RELIGIOUS SIGNS, SYMBOLS AND **SYMBOLISM** AND FOR GOOD REASON. THE ONLY TWO THINGS "GOING" IN THIS NEW WORLD WERE **MINING/EXPLORATION AND "RELIGION"**. EVERY SPANIARD AND MEXICAN IN ADDITION TO THE "RELIGIOUS" TRIED TO CONVERT SOULS AND **KNEW THE BIBLE** AND CHURCH TEACHING VERY WELL. THEREFORE, AS AN EXAMPLE, THE NUMBER "7" ON A MAP OR ALONG THE TRAIL SAYS: **HERE IS A CAMPSITE, AN OVERNIGHT RESTING PLACE**, TAKEN FROM THE BIBLE "... AND ON THE **7TH DAY HE RESTED**". ALSO, THE SYMBOL FOR NUMBER 1 IS A "DOT OR SOLID (FILLED IN) CIRCLE. THE SYMBOL FOR THE NUMBER ONE (1) IS ALSO THE SYMBOL FOR WATER/SPRINGS, AND AGAIN IS DERIVED FROM THE BIBLE, "ON THE FIRST DAY GOD CREATED WATER". THIS ABOVE INTRODUCTION IS TAKEN FROM THE BOOK: "TREASURE SIGNS, SYMBOLS, SHADOW AND SUN SIGNS" BY THE AUTHOR.

IF ONLY ACCURATE ARCHIVAL INFORMATION HAD BEEN AVAILABLE TO TREASURE HUNTERS BY "WRITERS OF TREASURE STORIES" REGARDING MEASUREMENTS/DISTANCES, SIGNS AND SYMBOL MEANINGS ON MAPS AND IN THE FIELD, PROBABLY A HUNDRED OR MORE TREASURES AND MINES WOULD HAVE BEEN FOUND BY NOW IN MEXICO AS WELL AS THE STATE OF ARIZONA WHICH IS ONE OF THE "RICHEST" STATES IN THE U.S.

A HORSE/ANIMAL CORRAL, **IF IT WAS CLOSE TO THE RANCH HOUSE**, WAS ONE OF THE VERY BEST HIDING PLACES BECAUSE THE ANIMALS' WEIGHT AND MOVEMENT WOULD QUICKLY PACK THE DIRT DOWN AFTER TREASURE WAS DEPOSITED OR RE-MOVED. ALSO YOU SHOULD CHECK OUT OLD "PIG STY" LOCATIONS.

UN CORRAL PAR UN CABALLO/ANIMAL, ESTABA CERCA DEL RANCHO, ERA UNO DE LOS MEJORES LUGARES, PORQUE LOS ANIMALS DESPUES DE DEPOSITO DEL TESORO ESTAMPAUAN LA TIERRA, TAMBIEN LUGARES DE PUERCOS

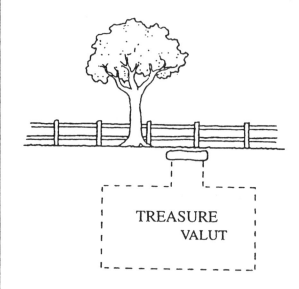

HORSE CORRAL

TREASURE VALUT

UNDER LARGE RANCH BARBEQUES WHERE THEY ROASTED SMALL CATTLE AND OTHER ANIMALS FOR "FIESTAS" AND SPECIAL OCCASIONS IS ANOTHER GREAT LOCATION USED BY MANY AS THEIR PRIVATE BANK. THIS ONE WAS A FAVORITE OF PANCHO VILLA.

DEBAJO DE UNA BARBACOA GRANDE DONDE ASAVAN GANADO PEQUENOS Y OTROS ANIMALS PARA "FIESTAS" Y OCASIONES ESPECIALES ES OTRA BUENA LOCALIDAD USADO POR MUCHOS, COMO BANCO PRIVADA ESTE ERA UN FAVORITO DE PANCHO VILLA

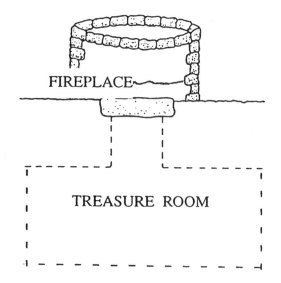

BARBEQUE

FIREPLACE

TREASURE ROOM

MANY ROCK WALLED WATER WELLS HAVE TREASURE ROOMS **IN USE TODAY** IN ISOLATED AREAS AROUND THE WORLD, ESPECIALLY **MEXICO**. THE ROCK COVERED ENTRANCE WILL USUALLY BE MID POINT BETWEEN THE GROUND LEVEL AND THE WATER LEVEL.

MUCHAS FUENTES DE AGUA CON PAREDES DE PIEDRA TANAN CUARTOS DE TESORO EN USO TODAVIA EN LUGARS ISLADO ALREDEDOR DEL MUNDO ESPECIALMENTE MEJICO. LA PUERTA ESTA LOCALIZADA EN EL MEDIO PUNTO DE AGUA Y LA TIERA.

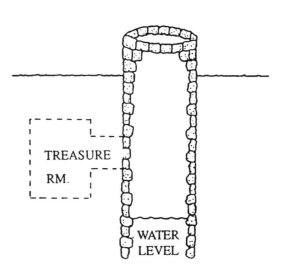

WATER WELL

TREASURE RM.

WATER LEVEL

UNDER AN OLD FIREPLACE WAS SURELY THE MOST COMMON HIDING PLACE FOR VALUABLES AND TREASURES. USUALLY A FIRE WAS ALWAYS LIT TO HEAT COFFEE, COOK AND HEAT THE ROOM, AND SELDOM WAS THIS LOCATION CHECKED BY THIEVES AND ROBBERS.

DEBAJO DE UN HORNO DE PIEDRA ERA UNO DE LOS MAS COMUN LUGARES PARA ESCONDER OBJETOS VALIOSOS Y TESOROS. LA LUMBRE ESTABA PARA EL CAFE, COMIDA Y CALENTADOR PARA EL CUARTO, Y LADRONES CASI NUNCA BUSCABAN EN LOS HORNOS.

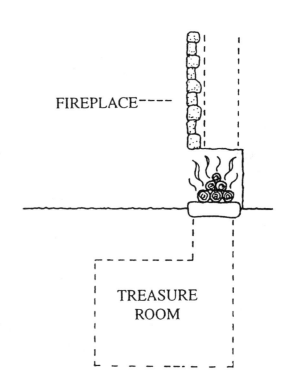

FIREPLACE----

TREASURE ROOM

GOLD: WHEN IN "PINE TREE COUNTRY" AND THE PINE CONES ARE HANGING, LOOK FOR TREES **WITHOUT** CONES OR CONES **ONLY** ON THE MAIN TRUNK. **ARSENIC** AND/OR **MERCURY** WHICH SURROUNDS, IN VARYING DEGREES, **ALL GOLD ORE BODIES** SEEMS TO AFFECT (THE VAPORS) PINE CONE TREES DIRECTLY.

SILVER: CONSTANTLY BE ON THE ALERT FOR THE "SULFIDE WEED". IT THRIVES AND SURVIVES **ONLY** AND EXCLUSIVELY WHERE SULFIDES PERCOLATE UP TO THE SURFACE. SOMETIMES A "PATCH" OR IRREGULAR LINE OF SULFIDE WEED WILL BE FOUND MEANDERING DOWN A HILLSIDE FOLLOWING A FAULT LINE OR VEIN. NOTE: THERE ARE SULFIDES OTHER THAN "SILVER SULFIDES" BUT IT'S SURE WORTH CHECKING.

FAULTS AND VEINS: ARE NOT ALWAYS INDICATED BY TOPOGRAPHIC WASHES AND DEPRESSION LINES. FAULTS USUALLY ACCUMULATE AND STORE FAR MORE MOISTURE/WATER THAN THE SURROUNDING AREA. THEREFORE, TREES, SAGUAROS, EVEN BRUSH, IF OVER OR ADJOINING, WILL BE OF **GREATER** SIZE, JUST AS THOSE ALONG A WASH OR STREAM ARE LARGER. LOOK FOR A TRAIL LINE OR GROUPING OF "FATTER" OR LARGER GROWTH.

SPANISH MINE AREA: LOOK FOR A **BARREN** AREA (AS RELATED TO THE SURROUNDING AREA) THAT IS RELATIVELY "FLAT". THIS COULD BE A "PATIO" WHERE THE MINERS USED "MERCURY" (BEGINNING IN THE 1560'S) TO RECOVER FROM LOW GRADE ORE. THE MERCURY COMPLETELY KILLS GROWTH AND "STUNTS" GROWTH AROUND THE AREA. NOTE: SOMETIMES BEDROCK A FEW FEET BELOW THE SURFACE OR A "BORAX" DEPOSIT ALSO WILL BE THE CAUSES OF A BARREN AREA.

SPANISH ADVICE: IN THE 1560'S AND 70'S SPAIN MADE MANY DRAWINGS AND WOODCUTS DEPICTING "HOW TO" DEVELOP MINES, SHORING, AIR VENTS, ETC. ALSO, THEY ISSUED A LIST OF ADVICE TO PROSPECTORS/EXPLORERS ON WHAT TO GIVE SPECIAL ATTENTION TO IN SEARCHING. HERE ARE A FEW: 1. SEARCH WHERE THE HILLS/MTNS. ARE THE **MOST RUGGED** ALONG THE

SKYLINE. 2. GIVE VERY SPECIAL ATTENTION TO A HALF LEAGUE RADIUS (1 MILE) OF ALL **"SPRINGS"** (FAULTS) 3. LOOK FOR AREAS OF "OVERSIZED TREES" HIGH IN THE MOUNTAINS. 4. LOOK FOR GROUND AREAS COLORED "ORANGE" OR "LIGHT GREEN" OR "BURNED OUT" IN COLOR.

DOWSING: IN THE EARLY 1500'S TO MID 1600'S THE SPANISH USED DOWSING RODS TO FIND GOLD AND SILVER ORE BODIES. THEY FELT THAT "DOWSING" WAS THE BEST WAY TO PROSPECT FOR SOME YEARS. THE SPANISH SEEMED TO BE VERY SUCCESSFUL IN FINDING ORE BODIES IN THIS MANNER FOR ABOUT 100 YEARS THEN THEY **SUDDENLY** TURNED TO MORE BASIC PROSPECTING METHODS. WE DON'T KNOW WHY THEY GAVE UP ON DOWSING BECAUSE IT SEEMINGLY WORKED FOR SOME SPANIARDS — MAYBE IT WOULD WORK FOR YOU.

TREASURE SHELTER ROCK: (ALSO SEE PAGE 44.) THESE LARGE "FREE STANDING" BOULDERS WERE ORIGINALLY CONSTRUCTED BY PIRATES AND USUALLY FACED THE OPEN SEA TO ADVISE THAT A "WEATHERPROTECTED" ANCHORAGE WAS AT THAT COASTLINE POINT. THE REVETMENT/RECESSED AREA CUT INTO THE BOULDER IS A PERFECT SHELTER FROM A **RAINSTORM** FOR ABOUT 4 TO 6 PERSONS. THE SPANISH USED THIS MONUMENT TO COVER MINE ENTRANCES IN SOME CASES; HOWEVER, MOST OF THE TIME IT WAS USED AS A "SHELTER" FOR TREASURES OR HIGH GRADE RICH ORE PLACED IN A DEEP HOLE UNDER THE CENTER OF THE BOULDER. ALSO, THIS MONUMENT WAS USED IN **FLATLAND AREAS** AS AN "ALPHA MONUMENT" AND THEN, OF COURSE, NOTHING WOULD BE UNDER IT AND IT WOULD SIMPLY BE A MESSAGE THAT FURTHER ON THE "OMEGA ROCK" WOULD BE FOUND WHICH WOULD LOOK THE SAME, YET **THIS ONE** WOULD ACTUALLY HIDE/SHELTER THE MINE ITSELF OR THE TREASURE.

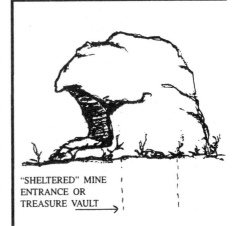

"SHELTERED" MINE ENTRANCE OR TREASURE VAULT →

THE MAJORITY OF ALL TREASURE/MINE MAP SYMBOLS ARE DERIVED FROM THE BIBLE. EARLY ON, THE JEWISH PEOPLE USED OLD TESTAMENT SIGNS, SYMBOLS AND REFERENCES TO HIDE MEANINGS FROM AN OPPRESSOR. THE EARLY CHURCH DID THE SAME AND DEVELOPED MORE THROUGHOUT THE YEARS. "RELIGIOUS" NUMEROLOGISTS WERE THE GREATEST OF MAP-MAKERS AND AT TIMES THEY WOULD DESIGN THE BASICS OF A "TREASURE MAP" OR HIDDEN MINE MAP BEFORE THE MINE WAS EVEN DISCOVERED OR THE TREASURE HIDDEN — AND THEN LATER "MAKE THE MINE/TREASURE FIT THE CODED MAP.

NUMEROUS MAPS WILL HAVE A DRAWING OF MATHEW, MARK, LUKE OR JOHN'S "CHURCH" SYMBOL. THE COMMON ONES ARE:

A "MAN WITH WINGS" REPRESENTS "MATHEW"

A "WINGED LION" REPRESENTS "MARK"

A "WINGED OXEN OR CALF" REPRESENTS "LUKE"

THE "EAGLE" REPRESENTS "JOHN"; ALSO, THE NUMBER "4" IS JOHN'S SYMBOL

IF ANY OF THESE FIGURES ARE ON A MAP IT TELLS YOU ONE OF TWO THINGS AND SOMETIMES BOTH:

A.   IF THE SYMBOL IS NEAR TWO TO FOUR NUMBERS, IT MEANS LOOK TO THE BIBLE, USING THE TWO TO FOUR NUMBERS TO FIND THE CHAPTER AND THE VERSE OF THE GOSPEL WRITTEN BY THAT FIGURE, THAT WILL TELL YOU THE DIRECTION, DISTANCE OR WHAT YOU NEED TO KNOW.

B.   MANY TIMES, IF ONE OF THESE SYMBOLS IS AT THE TOP, BOTTOM OR OFF TO THE SIDE OF THE MAP, IT IS SAYING THAT THIS "FIGURE" IS THE MAP-MAKERS PATRON OR THAT THE FIGURE IS THE PATRON OF THE MAP-MAKERS RELIGIOUS ORDER.

C. THE ONE SYMBOL THAT WAS MOST COMMONLY USED ON MAPS HERE IN THE U.S. AND IN **MEXICO** WAS THE **"EAGLE", "JOHN"**. ALSO, IT WAS THE ONLY SYMBOL THAT MIGHT BE FOUND AT THE MINE/TREASURE SITE BECAUSE IT TELLS A STORY WITHIN ITSELF AND GIVES DIRECTIONS: IF YOU FIND AN EAGLE CARVED, FOR EXAMPLE, ON A LARGE BOULDER, STAND FACING THE EAGLE, LOOK SLIGHTLY LEFT OF ITS WING TIP, THE ONE TO YOUR LEFT, THEN LOOK UP, DRAWING A MENTAL LINE UP-HILL OR WHEREVER THAT DIRECTION LEADS, FOR THAT IS WHERE THE TREASURE LAY, OR MAYBE ALONG THAT LINE YOU WILL FIND A FINAL MARKER. THE RELIGIOUS MEANING COMES FROM THE CRUCIFICATION, "JOHN" IS SHOWN STANDING AT THE FOOT OF THE CROSS. TO THE LEFT OF "JOHN" IS THE CROSS AND UP HIGH ON THE CROSS IS JESUS, HIGH ON JOHN'S LEFT. THUS: "HERE ON JOHN'S LEFT AND UP HIGHER IS THE "TREASURE" (JESUS). THE DOUBLE MEANING AND MESSAGE OF THE EAGLE SHOULD BE QUITE CLEAR TO A "BELIEVER" AND OF NO MEANING TO A NON-BELIEVER TRYING TO INTERPRET A CODED MAP.

KEEP IN MIND THAT IN GENERAL, THE CHURCH, THE "RELIGIOUS" AND THE BIBLICAL SCHOLARS THAT ASSISTED IN DESIGN-ING/CODING OF MAPS, DID SO BECAUSE THEY WERE WELL VERSED IN SYMBOLISM, ETC., AND WERE REQUESTED TO ASSIST BY MINE OWNERS AS WELL AS SPAIN. IT DOES NOT MEAN OR REFLECT IN ANY WAY THAT THEY OR THE "CHURCH" HELD ANY OWNERSHIP IN THE MAP, MINE OR TREASURE — BUT QUIEN SABE?

ONE THING IS CERTAIN IN REGARD TO THE CHURCH, MISSIONS AND MINING. BOTH THE SPANISH AND THE MEXICAN MINERS AND MINE OWNERS WERE ALWAYS VERY GENEROUS TO THE CHURCH AND THEY PAID FOR THE BUILDING AND FURNISHINGS OF MANY MISSIONS. IN SOME CASES THE MINE OWNERS ACTUALLY GAVE A SPECIFIC PERCENTAGE OF THEIR MINE'S INCOME TO THEIR LOCAL MISSION.

SOLID ROCK
MOUNTAINSIDE

CROSS/STATUE
HERE

IN THE PAST YEARS WE HAVE FOUND FIVE SHRINES. FOUR OF THE FIVE WERE SIMILAR TO THE ABOVE SKETCH. THE FIFTH WAS A CONVERTED CAVE. AT THE CAVE SHRINE, BY ACCIDENT, WE FOUND THE CARVED/CUT CANOPY ROCKS. THEY WERE ABOUT 1 ½ INCHES THICK AND TAPERED FROM 9 INCHES TO 14 INCHES WIDE. THEY WERE "RED" (HEMATITE), PROBABLY USED FOR ITS BEAUTY, AND WEIGHED ABOUT TWENTY-THREE POUNDS EACH.

MINE "SHRINES"

EVERY MINE HAD A SHRINE NEAR THE MINE'S ENTRANCE. EVEN A SMALL TWO TO FIVE MAN OPERATION HAD A NEARBY "PLACE" FOR DAILY PRAYERS. THE SHRINE USUALLY CONTAINED A SIMPLE CROSS, OR FOR A LARGE MINE IT COULD CONTAIN AS WELL AS A CROSS, A STATUE. MINE WORK WAS DANGEROUS AND A PRAYER SAID AT THE SHRINE BEFORE ENTERING THE MINE AND AGAIN UPON LEAVING TO SAY A PRAYER OF THANKSGIVING WAS A DAILY ROUTINE.

SUBJECT TO THE TERRAIN, THE SHRINE VARIED. IT COULD BE A NARROW SPACE BETWEEN LARGE ROCKS, OR A CAVE CONVERTED TO THE "FRAY'S/FRIAR'S" DAYTIME "CASA", WHICH THE MINERS PREFERRED BECAUSE THEN THE PADRE WOULD BE QUICKLY AVAILABLE TO ANY INJURED, AND HEAR THEIR LAST WORDS

BEFORE DYING. SPAIN'S LAW REQUIRED THE SHRINE TO BE **WITHIN 200 VARAS** (WALKING/SOLDIERS) OF THE MINE'S ENTRANCE.

A SHRINE WAS USUALLY 3 TO 5 FEET WIDE, ONLY 2 TO 2 ½ FEET DEEP AND 4 TO 6 FEET HIGH. THE TOP OF THE SHRINE WAS ALWAYS CURVED. FREQUENTLY A CANOPY WAS SET ALONG THE RADIUS OF THE CURVE AND PROJECTED OUT FROM THE WALL ABOUT 10 INCHES, MADE EITHER OF WOOD OR STONE. IF YOU FIND HOLES HAVE BEEN DRILLED ALONG THE TOP (CURVE) OF A POSSIBLE SHRINE, THEN YOU KNOW FOR SURE.

THE MINERS REMOVED THE CANOPY PIECES AND THE CROSS/STATUE AND HID THEM NEARBY WHEN DEPARTING FOR A PERIOD OF TIME. THE KNEELING AREA MAY BE AS LARGE AS FORTY FEET SQUARE.

SMALL TWO TO FIVE MAN SPANISH AND MEXICAN TUNNEL MINES FREQUENTLY HAD A FAIR SIZED "ROOM" ABOUT 15 FEET INTO THE TUNNEL THAT SERVED MANY PURPOSES SUCH AS STORING TOOLS, WATER JUGS, FOOD, ETC., AS WELL AS A LARGE SHELF OR NITCH IN A SIDE WALL THAT HELD A STATUE OR CRUCIFIX AND CANDLE WHICH SERVED AS THEIR "SHRINE".

THE HIDING PLACE OF GOLD AND SILVER ORE AND BARS IN A SMALL TUNNEL MINE USUALLY WAS IN THE ROOM'S **FLOOR DIRECTLY BELOW THE LEDGE** OR NITCH (SHRINE) IN HOPES THAT THE SHRINE WOULD "PROTECT" THEIR PROPERTY. THE OTHER IMPORTANT LOCATION TO CHECK FOR TREASURE IN **TUNNELS AND CAVES** IS IMMEDIATELY AT THE ENTRANCE TO THE CAVE AND TUNNEL. MANY TIMES **AT THE ENTRANCE** TO A CAVE WHERE MINERS MAY HAVE LIVED YOU WILL FIND A ROW OF ROCKS. THESE ROCKS WERE HEATED IN THE EVENING AND PLACED AT THE CAVE'S DOORWAY TO KEEP OUT SNAKES AND OTHER UNWELCOME VISITORS. IT IS UNDER THESE ROCKS WHERE A "SLOT" HOLE WAS DUG TO HIDE THEIR TREASURES.

THE **LARGEST** SIGN, SYMBOL, NUMBER, WORD OR FIGURE ON A MAP IS USUALLY THE "KEY" OR "CLUE" TO THE CODE OF THE MAP OR THE MAP MAKER. BE ALERT TO ANY LETTERS IN A WORD THAT ARE SOMEWHAT LARGER, OR SMALLER, THAN THE OTHER LETTERS IN THE WORD. OF GREATEST IMPORTANCE IS TO CHECK EVERY LETTER "A" TO SEE IF ITS CROSS BAR IS ANGLED. THE LETTER "A" IS A SPANISH **WORD** AND MEANS: "GO - TO - AT." SEE "CODED LETTER/DOCUMENTS TO TREASURE."

MEXICO'S "CODES" WERE PRETTY MUCH THE SAME AS THE SPANISH WITH MINOR CHANGES. THESE WERE COMPILED IN 1826 AND DURING MEXICO'S 26 YEAR REIGN OVER WHAT IS NOW THE UNITED STATES. MEXICO WAS NOT ABLE TO ENFORCE MANY MINING RULES. MOST MEXICAN MINING FAMILIES OR HACIENDAS USED THE "OLD" CODES AND EITHER ADDED OR CHANGED A FEW FOR "FAMILY ONLY" UNDERSTANDING.

KEEP IN MIND THAT THE SPANISH (IN SPAIN) HAD BEEN CONQUERED BY ROME AND INUNDATED BY THE "MOORS" SO BOTH ROMAN AND ARABIC INFLUENCES, WRITING, WORDS AND **NUMBERS** WERE WELL KNOWN AND COMMONLY USED OR INTERCHANGED BY THE SPANISH ON MAPS, LETTERS AND DOCUMENTS.

NO MARKS, SIGNS OR "INDICATORS" WILL EVER BE FOUND **DIRECTLY** OVER OR "ON THE TOP OF" A MINE ENTRANCE OR TREASURE. THIS WAS A CARDINAL RULE OF THE SPANISH AND CONTINUED BY **MEXICANS**, NOT THE SLIGHTEST OR SMALLEST MARK WAS ALLOWED AT THE **EXACT** HIDING SPOT. BECAUSE OF THIS LAW, "TRIANGLES" WERE THE FAVORITE MARKERS OF THE SPANISH AND WERE CONSTRUCTED NEAR MINE/TREASURE LOCATIONS, TO BE USED AS THE "BASE" FOR EXACT MEASURING TO THIS MINE/TREASURE.

IF YOU FEEL THAT YOU "KNOW" WHAT AREA THE MAP DESCRIBES OR DEPICTS, YET THE TOPOGRAPHY JUST DOES NOT SEEM TO FIT, FLIP THE MAP UPSIDE DOWN, "NORTH" MAY BE

"SOUTH", SOMETIMES A "RIO" MAY NOT BE A RIVER BUT A SEASONAL STREAM OR WASH OR PUT THE MAP UP TO A MIRROR AND VIEW IT IN REVERSE. MIRROR/WATER IMAGE MAPS WERE COMMON. IF NOT THE FULL MAP, THEN A **PORTION** OF THE MAP COULD BE **MIRROR IMAGE**.

SIGNS, SYMBOLS AND NUMBERS WERE USED **MORE THAN ONCE (RE-USED)** WHENEVER POSSIBLE ON A MAP TO ACHIEVE MORE THAN ONE MEANING OR MESSAGE.

THE ALPHA AND THE OMEGA (THE **ALL IMPORTANT** SPANISH MONUMENT **IN THE FIELD**). **ANY** SPANISH TREASURE/HIDDEN MINE **CAN BE FOUND WITHOUT A DETECTOR OR ANY ELECTRONICS IF YOU FIND THE "ALPHA" FIRST, BECAUSE THE OMEGA IS AT THE MINE/TREASURE — AND IS IDENTICAL, THE SAME AS THE ALPHA MONUMENT.** THUS FULFILLING AND REFLECTING THE BIBLICAL QUOTE OF "I AM THE ALPHA AND THE OMEGA", I AM THE BEGINNING AND END, "I AM THE FIRST AND THE FINAL". THE SPANISH, IN ADDITION TO PLACING/CON-STRUCTING MONUMENTS TO AND FROM THE MINE AND/OR TREASURE, WERE REQUIRED BY SPAIN **TO INSTALL ALPHAS AND OMEGAS**.

IF THE "ALPHA" (TRAIL ENTRANCE MONUMENT) IS IN THE SHAPE OF A **HEART**, THERE WILL BE ANOTHER "HEART" (THE "OMEGA") AT THE MINE/TREASURE. **WHATEVER THE SHAPE/FORM OF THE ALPHA MONUMENT IS,** IT WILL BE REPEATED (THE SAME) AT THE **END OF THE TRAIL**. THE "ALPHA" MONUMENT COULD BE OF ANY DESIGN — IT MAY BE AN INDIAN HEAD, A TREASURE SHELTER ROCK, A LARGE "X", A HORSE'S HEAD, ETC. ETC. — WHATEVER WAS EASIEST TO CONSTRUCT AND MATCH WITH THE GEOLOGY AT THE BEGINNING OF THE TRAIL AND AT THE END.

AN ARCHIVIST (OF ROME) TOLD ME THE FOLLOWING STORY. IT SEEMS THAT A CERTAIN "KING" OF SPAIN, IN THE MID 1500'S HAD A VERY HIGH OPINION OF HIS PHYSICAL SIZE AND SHAPE. THE KING WAS INVOLVED IN ADJUSTING AND SETTING UP "SPAIN'S MEASURING SYSTEM" **FOR MINES AND TREASURES ONLY**, SO – NATURALLY – HE CALLED IN HIS **TAILOR** TO ASSIST IN THIS GREAT MATTER AT HAND. FIVE OF THE SIX "ROYAL" MEASUREMENTS FOLLOW: 1. BRAZA 5'7", THE DISTANCE BETWEEN FINGERTIPS WITH THE KING'S ARM OUTSTRETCHED. 2. ESTADO 5'7", THE HEIGHT OF A MAN (HIS). 3. VARA 33", HIS WAIST LINE AND STEP DISTANCE (HEEL TO TOE) 4. CODO (½ VARA) 16 ½", FROM THE POINT OF HIS ELBOW TO THE POINT OF HIS LITTLE FINGER (OUTSTRETCHED). 5. PALMO 8 1/4", THE DISTANCE BETWEEN THE TIP OF HIS LITTLE FINGER AND THUMB'S TIP WHEN HIS PALM/HAND WAS SPREAD OPEN. THIS ARCHIVIST HAD NOT HIMSELF SEEN THIS DOCUMENT, BUT WAS INFORMED BY ANOTHER ARCHIVIST OF ITS EXISTENCE. AN INTERESTING STORY I FELT, AND MORE SO BECAUSE THESE SPECIALIZED "ROYAL" MEASUREMENTS ARE THE **EXCLUSIVE** MEASUREMENTS USED ON SPAIN'S TREASURE MAPS. SPAIN'S LAW REQUIRES THESE MEASUREMENTS TO BE USED ON ALL TREASURE/MINE MAPS IN THE NEW WORLD AND **NEVER** TO CHANGE. (PERU, COLOMBIA, PANAMA, GUATEMALA, MEXICO, ETC.)

IT IS TRUE THAT SPAIN TWICE CHANGED MEASUREMENTS AND DISTANCES DURING ITS 350-YEAR RULE OF THE NEW WORLD; HOWEVER, THE CHANGES HAD **NO EFFECT ON TREASURE MAPS AND MINE MAPS MEASUREMENTS**. THE FOLLOWING MEASURE-MENTS REMAINED **CONSTANT**.

LEAGUE	THE NAUTICAL LEAGUE WAS 3.27 MILES AND THE VARIABLE, BECAUSE OF CURRENT (BOAT DRIFT), WAS CONSIDERED TO BE 3.18 TO 3.27. THE STATUTE (LAND) LEAGUE WAS 2.18 MILES; THE VARIABLE WAS CONSIDERED TO BE 2.1 TO 2.18. TWO NAUTICAL LEAGUES WERE APPROXIMATED TO EQUAL THREE STATUTE LEAGUES. NAUTICAL = OCEAN, STATUTE = LAND.
BRAZA	THE BRAZA WAS 5 FEET 7 INCHES, USED PRIMARILY FOR WATER DEPTHS. TODAY THE FATHOM IS USED, WHICH IS 6 FEET. SAILORS AND PIRATES USED "BRAZAS" AS MEASURING DISTANCES WHEN BURIALS OF TREASURES WERE MADE ON ISLANDS OR ALONG COASTLINES. THEIR TREASURE MAPS SELDOM MEANT PACES OR VARAS, EVEN THOUGH THE MAP MIGHT SAY **"PLACES"**.
UN ESTADO	"UN ESTADO" WAS KNOWN AS THE HEIGHT OF A MAN, 5 FEET 7 INCHES, AND REFERRED TO DEPTH IN THE GROUND. COVERED AND HIDDEN MINES, AS WELL AS MAJOR TREASURES WERE TO BE COVERED TO "UN ESTADO" OR IF BURIED DEEPER IN MULTIPLES OF "UN ESTADOS". A "BRAZA" WAS THE NAUTICAL EQUIVALENT IN LENGTH.
VARA	THIS IS THE TOUGH ONE, THERE WERE MANY MANY "VARA" DISTANCES, EACH STATE AND PROVINCE OF SPAIN HAD THEIR OWN MEASUREMENTS FOR A VARA, SO, SOME MAPS OF THE SPANISH MAY USE THEIR LOCAL HOMELAND MEASUREMENT, 30" TO 35.9". HERE, TREASURE/MINE MAPS WERE TO BE: THE WALKING (SOLDIERS) VARA IS **APPROXIMATELY** 33". THE MEASURED VARA IS **EXACTLY** 33".

CODO	THE "CODO" WAS HALF OF A VARA – 16 ½". THIS MAINLY RELATED TO WATER DEPTH IN TREASURE REPORTS/DOCUMENTS AND SOMETIMES ON MAPS WHERE A GALLEON OR TREASURE BOAT SUNK. **NOTE:** ALL REPORTED WATER DEPTHS WERE ALWAYS MEASURED FROM **HIGH TIDE**.
PALMO	THE "PALMO" WAS HALF OF A "CODO" – 8 1/4". ITS APPEARANCE ON A TREASURE MAP WAS USUALLY SIMPLY TO DESCRIBE OR TELL THE SIZE OF GOLD OR SILVER BARS. ALSO, FREQUENTLY THE "PALMO" WAS USED TO TELL THE DEPTH OF A STREAM OR RIVER THAT HAD PLACER GOLD.
MEXICO VARA	THE MEXICAN VARA WAS FIRMLY ESTABLISHED ON JANUARY 4, 1823, AFTER SPAIN'S RULE, AT 32.8 INCHES. HOWEVER, BECAUSE OF MEXICO'S CONSTANT TURMOIL AND DISORGANIZED OVERSEEING OF MOST MINERS/MINES, THE OLD SIGNS, SYMBOLS **AND** MEASUREMENTS WERE STILL USED. AT THIS TIME MANY NEW SIGNS OR NEW SIGN MEANINGS WERE PRIVATELY ADDED TO "FAMILY" HELD MAPS.
PLACES-DISTANCES	"PLACES" AND "DISTANCES" WHEN EITHER OF THESE WORDS ARE USED ON A MAP OR TREASURE DOCUMENT IT USUALLY TELLS YOU THAT: A. THE MEASUREMENTS ARE **NOT** IN VARA DISTANCES B. IF A "RELIGIOUS" MADE THE MAP, IT MAY BE A COMMON DISTANCE KNOWN TO **HIS** HOMELAND, OF GERMANY, FRANCE OR ITALY, ETC.

1. GOLD, SILVER AND SAND BARS

CAPTAIN ISRAEL GRAY, AN INDEPENDENT FRENCHMAN OF SPAIN AND OWNER OF A GOOD SHIP, WORKED ALONG THE WEST COAST AND IN THE GULF OF CALIFORNIA. HE TRANSPORTED MINERS, MINING EQUIPMENT AND JUST ABOUT ANYTHING NEEDED BETWEEN 1846 AND 1862. CAPTAIN GRAY KNEW MANY MINERS AND WAS KNOWN AS A BUYER, IF THE PRICE WAS RIGHT, OF RICH HIGHGRADED (STOLEN) GOLD AND SILVER ORE FROM MINERS. CAPTAIN GRAY HAD CONVERTED HIS ORE TO 60 TO 80 POUND BARS WHICH HE INTENDED TO TAKE WITH HIM WHEN HE LEFT MEXICAN WATERS AND RETURNED TO SPAIN — BUT PROBLEMS CAME UP IN 1862 AND HE HAD TO DEPART MEXICO ON SHORT NOTICE AND COULD NOT RECOVER HIS BURIED TREASURE. CAPTAIN GRAY DIED SOME YEARS LATER IN SPAIN AND IN HIS OLD SHIP'S LOG BOOK WAS FOUND A LONG LETTER HE HAD WRITTEN. HERE IS THE TREASURE LOCATION INFORMATION:

DEAR KINSMAN:

"...YES, I NOT ONLY FEARED THE TIME IT WOULD REQUIRE TO UNCOVER MY TREASURE AND THE DEPARTURE DELAY IT WOULD CAUSE, I HAVE FEARED GOING BACK FOR IT AND DISTRUSTED OTHERS TO GET IT FOR ME. IT IS YOURS – 16 GOLD BARS AND 38 SILVER BARS BURIED ON A VERY SMALL 3 ACRE ISLAND MUCH LIKE A SAND BAR ON THE BALUARTE RIVER NOT FAR FROM THE GULF OF CALIFORNIA COASTLINE, BETWEEN THE GULF AND ROSARIO, SINALOA, MEXICO, (WHICH IS ABOUT 40 MILES SOUTH OF MAZATLAN). THE BURIAL IS NEAR THE LOWER END OF THE ISLAND MID POINT BETWEEN TWO FAIR SIZED TREES. POSSIBLY CONSIDER, AS I DID, TO APPROACHING THE CHURCH WITH AN OFFER OF SHARING EQUALLY IF THEY WOULD PROTECT YOU AND SHIP YOU BACK THERE WITH SOME OF THEIR PADRES TO MAKE THE RECOVERY." NOTE: IF THE TREASURE IS STILL THERE I WOULD THINK THAT A 3 OR 4 DAY "FISHING" TRIP

UP BALUARTE RIVER WITH A COUPLE OF METAL DETECTORS MIGHT PAY OFF BIGTIME.

2. GOLD ORE DUMP AS BIG AS A HOUSE

IN A CANYON BELOW "LA MESA ENCANTADA" (THE ENCHANTED TABLELAND) THAT HAS VERY STEEP AND HIGH WALLS LIES A GIANT PILE OF RICH GOLD ORE THE SIZE OF A HOUSE. SUPPLIES FOR THE MINE AND THE MINERS WERE BROUGHT UP THE GULF OF CALIFORNIA TO A COASTLINE POINT 93 MILES SOUTH OF THE GULF'S HEAD, FROM WHICH THE MINERS WOULD CARRY THE SUPPLIES INLAND TO THE MINE, A DAY AND A HALF TRIP. A MINOR REVOLUTION BROKE OUT AND THE BOAT THAT TOOK SUPPLIES TO THE MINERS WAS TAKEN BY SOME OFFICIALS FOR OTHER USE. THE MINERS DECIDED TO WALK OUT AFTER ABOUT SIX MONTHS OF NO SUPPLIES BEING DELIVERED. THEY ALL TOOK SOME GOLD ORE WITH THEM AND FOLLOWED A MAJOR CANYON ALL THE WAY TO THE GULF COAST AND THEN ON TO THE CLOSEST COMMUNITY "GUAYMAS". OFFICIALS IN GUAYMAS IMMEDIATELY ARRESTED THEM, TOOK THEIR GOLD ORE AND SHIPPED THEM OFF. THEIR STORY WAS WELL RECORDED BUT THE MINE AND "CASA" SIZED PILE OF ORO IS STILL UNFOUND. THE MINE IS IN A LARGE CANYON THAT HEADED NEAR THE EAST END OF THE MESA. IT'S RUGGED COUNTRY, A SMALL PLANE OR INFRA-RED MIGHT FIND THE SPOT.

3. PIRATE TREASURE

PIRATE TREASURE WAS BURIED NEAR THE NORTH BANK OF RIO SONORA LESS THAN 5 MILES IN FROM THE GULF OF CALIFORNIA. IT IS POSSIBLE THAT THE SERI INDIANS REMOVED IT AND RE-HID THIS TREASURE ON TIBURON. HOWEVER, IF IT'S STILL THERE, IT SHOULD BE FAIRLY EASY TO FIND. A LARGE FLAT FACED BOULDER OR CLIFF SIDE FACING THE RIO HAS A FOUR BRAZA (23') DIAMETER ANCHOR SYMBOL CUT INTO IT AND IS LESS THAN 300 FEET FROM THE RIVER'S NORTH BANKS. THE PORTUGUESE PIRATE SHIP'S PILOT TOLD OF THIS TREASURE TO

THE PADRE THAT HEARD HIS LAST CONFESSION BEFORE HE WAS HUNG FOR PIRACY TWO YEARS AFTER THE TREASURE WAS BURIED.

4. SEA OF CORTEZ TREASURE

RIO YAQUI ALSO HIDES A TREASURE OF GOLD AND SILVER BARS AND IS WITHIN TWO MILES OF THE GULF OF CALIFORNIA AND WITHIN 200 PACES OF WHERE THE RIO YAQUI NARROWS AND ACROSS FROM THE OLD JESUIT MISSION (CABECERA) "RAHUN", JUST WEST OF THE VISTA "POTAM". THESE BARS CAME FROM THE MINES **FAR** UP THE RIO YAQUI AND WERE AWAITING TRANSHIPMENT BY BOAT. THE YAQUI REBELLION CAUSED THE OFFICIALS TO TRANSFER THE STORED TREASURE TO A NEARBY CAVE LOCATION AND THEN BLASTED IT CLOSED. THE REPORTED MAIN REASON THAT THEY MOVED THE TREASURE WAS TO PROVE TO THE BOAT OFFICIALS THAT THEY HAD NOTHING FOR SHIPMENT, THUS INSURING ENOUGH ROOM ON THE BOAT TO TAKE ALL THE GUARDS, OFFICIALS, MINERS AND THEIR FAMILIES THAT HAD GATHERED AT THE GULF COAST AWAITING RESCUE. THE CAVE OF BARS WAS NEVER FOUND. DEEP DOUBLE-ENDERS OR GROUND PENETRATING RADAR SHOULD FIND IT TODAY — GO FOR IT!

5. 100 MILLION UNDER A SWIMMING POOL

"I HAVE ENOUGH TREASURE TO SUPPORT A FULL REVOLUTION IN MEXICO". THIS QUOTE IS ATTRIBUTED TO GENERAL ANACLETO LOPEZ (DIED IN 1970). "AND WITH MY AMIGO GENERAL BANUELOS OF VALVERDE WE COULD PAY FOR TWO REVOLUTIONS". IT SEEMS THAT THESE TWO GENERALS WERE WEALTHY EARLY ON, BUT IN 1943 ANACLETO TALKED WITH ONE OF HIS OLD GENERAL FRIENDS MANUEL AVILLA CAMACHO, WHO AT THAT TIME WAS THE PRESIDENT OF MEXICO. ANACLETO AT THAT TIME WAS IN FULL POWER AS GENERAL OF DIVISION. HE ASKED PRESIDENT CAMACHO TO REIMBURSE HIM FOR ALL THE MONEY HE SPENT ON HIS OWN TROOPS FOR SO MANY YEARS. SOON

AFTERWARD CAMACHO SENT **TWO ARMY TRUCKS WITH GOLD BARS** TO ANACLETO AT HIS HOME IN VIBORAS, "HACIENDA LAS VIBORAS".

THE TREASURE REMAINED ABOUT A WEEK AT THIS FAMILY HACIENDA AND THEN ANACLETO MOVED IT TO HIS **OTHER** HACIENDA NOT FAR AWAY BUT NOT BEFORE HIS FAMILY, INCLUDING **HIS SON ANACLETO JR.**, SAW THE TREASURE. THEREAFTER, THE GENERAL BUILT A CONCRETE SWIMMING POOL (ABOVE GROUND) AT HIS SECOND HACIENDA THAT HOUSED HIS MISTRESS. SPANISH TREASURE, A HUGE SAFE 4'X5'X8' AND CAMACHO'S GOLD IS HIDDEN AT THIS SECOND HACIENDA. HE HAD TOLD ANACLETO JR. THAT "ONE DAY SOON I WILL SHOW YOU WHERE THE TESOROS ARE HIDDEN" — BUT HE DIED IN HIS SLEEP AND NO ONE KNOWS WHERE IT IS. MAYBE **UNDER** THE SWIMMING POOL? ALSO, HOW ABOUT TREASURE AT GENERAL BANUELOS' OLD HACIENDA IN VALVERDE? **MAKE A DEAL** WITH THE FAMILIES OF THE ABOVE GENERALS — AND OTHER FAMILIES OF POLITICAL OFFICIALS AND GENERALS THAT HAVE PASSED AWAY. I BET THAT MOST OF THEM HAD SOME TREASURE HIDDEN AWAY, BECAUSE **NOBODY** TRUSTED BANKS.

6. PEAR SIZED GOLD NUGGETS

THERE IS A LAKE ON THE WESTERLY SIDE OF THE RIVER YAQUI, BETWEEN THE STATES OF SONORA AND CHIHUAHUA IN THE SIERRA MADRE MOUNTAINS. ADJOINING THE LAKE IS AN ANCIENT FURNACE WITH A SILVER AND COPPER SLAG MOUND CLOSE BY. TWO GOLD NUGGETS THE SIZE OF **PEARS** WERE FOUND WITH TOOLS NEAR THE FURNACE. THE MINE MUST BE CLOSE BY — BUT NEVER FOUND. "IT LOOKED AS THOUGH THEY LEFT IN A HURRY AND NEVER CAME BACK," SAID THE REPORT FILED BY ENRICO MARTINEZ, FEDERAL REPRESENTATIVE.

7. MONTEZUMA'S TREASURE

MONTEZUMA'S HIDDEN TREASURES ARE SAID BY MANY WRITERS TO BE IN UTAH, NEW MEXICO, ARIZONA AND OTHER UNITED STATES LOCATIONS. OUR RESEARCH INDICATES IT IS IN MEXICO, **SOUTH OF MONTEREY**. SOME FACTS TO CONSIDER:

1. A FEW OF THE TORTURED AZTECS GAVE THE **SAME** INFORMATION THAT THE CARAVAN OF TREASURE WENT NORTHERLY FROM MEXICO CITY FOR 43 DAYS THEN TURNED WESTERLY NEAR A GREAT LAKE AND TRAVELED 4½ MORE DAYS INTO A GREAT LONG CANYON IN THE MIDDLE OF A HUGE MOUNTAIN RANGE THAT HAD **SEVEN** (7) HIGH PEAKS. NEAR THE END OF THE LONG CANYON WERE **SEVEN** CAVES THAT HAD BEEN CLOSED AND HIDDEN. THEY REOPENED THESE CAVES, FILLED THEM WITH THE TREASURES AND RESEALED THEM. THEIR RETURN TRIP TOOK HALF THE TIME AND THEY WERE GONE FOR ABOUT 6 MONTHS.

2. THE SPANISH COULD TRAVEL ABOUT 32 MILES A DAY WITHOUT CARRYING EXCESSIVE WEIGHT SO THEY FIGURED THAT THE AZTECS TRAVELED 15 MILES A DAY GOING AND 30 MILES A DAY RETURNING AND THAT THE TREASURE WAS 275 LEAGUES (605 MILES) NORTHERLY AND THEN 29 LEAGUES (63 MILES) WESTERLY INTO THE MOUNTAIN RANGE.

3. WE **MUST** KEEP IN MIND THAT A SOLDIER'S OR WALKING LEAGUE WAS 2.18 STATUTE MILES (**NOT** 3 OR 3.5).

4. WE SPOKE WITH A FEW OF THE STAFF MEMBERS AND CARTOGRAPHERS (MAP MAKERS) OF THE ANTHROPOLOGY MUSEUM IN MEXICO CITY AND THEY GAVE US THEIR **THOUGHTS AND ADVICE** ON THE POSSIBLE OLD TRAILS TAKEN BY THE AZTECS TO HIDE THIS **UNBELIEVABLE TREASURE**. THIS LOCATION IS 150 MILES S.S.E. (SOUTH

SOUTH EAST) OF **"MONTEREY"** IN THE UPPER HALF OF SECTION 132 OF O.N.C. MAP J-24 AND DIRECTLY **WEST** OF THE **SOUTH** END OF THE **GREAT LAKE**.

8. ESCAPED PRISONER'S MINE

IN THE BEGINNING, ALL OF THE SANTA EVLALIA MINES IN CHIHUAHUA GAVE AN AMOUNT EQUAL TO 1/64TH OF THEIR OPERATION TO THE CATHEDRAL OF THE CITY OF CHIHUAHUA ANNUALLY FOR OVER 100 YEARS — PLUS **ORIGINALLY** DONATING OVER 1½ MILLION FOR THE MISSION'S CONSTRUCTION IN 1790. TODAY THE CHURCH STILL RECEIVES AN ANNUAL GIFT OF 1/64TH FROM **ONE** OF THE SURVIVING MINES. IN THE LATE 1800's EIGHT MEN BROKE OUT OF PRISON AND FLED TO THE MINERALIZED HIGH HILLS OF THE WILDERNESS AREA **BEYOND** THESE ESTABLISHED MINES AND LOCATED A **NEW** MINE. MEXICO OFFERED REWARDS TO THE INDIANS TO FIND THEM BUT NO RESULTS. ABOUT 15 YEARS LATER AN INDIAN REPRESENTING THE ESCAPEES CAME TO THE MISSION AND SPOKE WITH THE PADRE. "THE MEN REQUIRED FORGIVENESS FROM THE CHURCH AND FROM SPAIN AND WOULD GIFT THE PADRE AND THE GOVERNMENT **EACH** OVER ONE MILLION IN SILVER ORE". WITHIN SIX MONTHS THE AGREEMENT WAS MADE AND PAID. THE FORGIVEN MEN LIVED WELL FOR AWHILE THEREAFTER AND ANNUALLY WENT TO THEIR OLD MINE AREA AND QUIETLY BROUGHT BACK MANY OF THE SILVER BARS THEY HAD HIDDEN. THEN AN APACHE UPRISING OVERRAN THE TOTAL AREA AND KILLED ALL EIGHT MEN AS WELL AS MANY OTHERS. LITTLE IS KNOWN EXCEPT THE GENERAL LOCATION OF THEIR OLD MINE AND NEARBY HIDDEN HOARD OF SILVER BARS THAT ARE STILL WAITING TO BE FOUND. FINDING THIS ONE WILL SURELY TAKE SOME RESEARCH. I WOULD START WITH A VISIT TO THE CATHEDRAL, TALK WITH THE PADRE, CHECK THEIR ARCHIVES BETWEEN 1877 AND 1883 AND OF COURSE SAY A FEW PRAYERS.

9. PANCHO VILLA'S TREASURE

PANCHO VILLA'S HIDDEN TREASURES ARE SAID TO BE IN CALIFORNIA, ARIZONA, TEXAS AND MEXICO AND SOME MAY BE HIDDEN IN THOSE LOCATIONS — **BUT** HIS **MAJOR HIDDEN TREASURES** OF MEXICAN AND AMERICAN GOLD COINS, BARS OF GOLD, SILVER AND JEWELRY ARE HIDDEN IN THE STATE OF DURANGO, MEXICO. PRESIDENT DE LA HUERTA COULD NOT ELIMINATE PANCHO VILLA SO HE GAVE HIM THE STATE OF DURANGO TO **RULE** AS HE DESIRED FOR THE ANNUAL PAYMENT OF 4 TO 5 MILLION PESOS. PANCHO'S TREASURES WERE GATHERED FROM ALL PLACES POSSIBLE AND DELIVERED TO NORTHERN MEXICO AND HIDDEN IN THE SIERRA MADRE MOUNTAINS OF SONORA. PANCHO VILLA WAS KILLED BY THE FOLLOWING PRESIDENT OF MEXICO'S ORDERS, ALVARO OBREGON. THE PROBLEM IS THAT PANCHO HAD 4 OR POSSIBLY 5 HACIENDAS IN SONORA AND HE PLACED ¾ OF HIS TREASURES WITHIN 500 VARAS OF ONE HACIENDA IN A CAVE AND THE REMAINING ¼ OF HIS TREASURE WAS PUT UNDER A TREE IN THE CENTER OF A HORSE CORRAL ADJOINING ANOTHER OF HIS HACIENDAS ACCORDING TO ONE OF PANCHO'S GENERALS WHO FLED MEXICO TO EL PASO IMMEDIATELY WHEN PANCHO VILLA WAS KILLED IN 1923. ONE OF PANCHO VILLA'S HACIENDAS WAS AT CANUTILLO, DURANGO, AND ANOTHER AT CHIHUAHUA, CHIHUAHUA.

10. AZTEC VILLAGE TREASURE

THE SPANISH HEARD OF GREAT RICHES, GOLD, SILVER AND JADE POSSESSED BY A VILLAGE OF AZTECS IN INTENDENCIA DE SONORA, STATE OF SINALOA. THE SPANISH HIRED BLACK STEPHEN, THE MOOR AS THEIR GUIDE TO REACH THE VILLAGE. THE AZTECS FOUGHT WELL BUT WERE DEFEATED. SOME AZTECS ESCAPED, TAKING BLACK STEPHEN AND A FEW OTHERS AS PRISONERS. THE FEW AZTECS THAT REMAINED ALIVE TOLD THAT THEY HAD HEARD THE SPANISH WERE COMING AND HID ALL OF THEIR TREASURE IN A HUGE CAVE, A HALF A DAY'S WALKING

DISTANCE (15-16 MILES) FROM THE VILLAGE. THE CAVE IS LOCATED AT THE BEGINNING EDGE OF A VALLEY THAT IS **SIX LEAGUES (12½-13 MILES) LONG**. RESEARCH IN CHOIX AND STUDY TOPO MAPS SEARCHING FOR A 12/13 MILE LONG VALLEY.

11. 3¼ LEAGUE CANAL TO TREASURE

YAQUI INDIANS REVEALED TO THE SPANISH A FABULOUS RICH GOLD MINE SOUTHEAST OF "MATEHUALA" VERY NEAR VACATETE MOUNTAIN, MEXICO, ABOUT 4 LEAGUES (8.6 MILES) EASTERLY OF CERRO AZUL. WATER FOR ARRASTRES WAS NOT AVAILABLE SO A 3¼ LEAGUE (7 MILES) CANAL WAS DUG TO BRING WATER TO THE ARRASTRES AND INTO A LARGE POND OR SMALL LAKE ADJOINING THE MINERS' CAMPGROUNDS. THE CANAL ENDED AT THE ONLY PERMANENT BUILDING, A SMALL ADOBE CHURCH. AN INDIAN UPRISING KILLED THE SPANISH, CLOSED THE MINE WITH HUNDREDS OF GOLD BARS INSIDE, DEMOLISHED THE CAMP AND CHURCH BUILDING BUT DID NOT REFILL THE 7 MILE LONG CANAL THAT CAME FROM THE NEARBY MOUNTAINS. FIND AND FOLLOW THE CANAL TO THE POND/LAKE, THEN FOLLOW THE MONUMENTS AND TRAILMARKERS TO THE MINE.

12. 50 YEARS OF TREASURE

A CONVERTED INDIAN BECAME THE GREATEST BENEFACTOR TO THE CHURCH OF NUESTRA SENORA DE LA GUADALUPE IN JUAREZ, JUST ACROSS FROM EL PASO. THE INDIAN WOULD BRING MUCH GOLD AND SILVER TO THE CHURCH PADRE FOUR TO SIX TIMES A YEAR. HE TOLD THE PADRE THAT HE COULD SEE THE CHURCH FROM HIS MINE/CAVE AND THAT THERE WERE MANY, MANY OLD BAGS OF ORO IN ONE OF THE "ROOMS". THE INDIAN DIED WITHOUT REVEALING THE LOCATION TO THE PADRE. THE INDIAN TOLD THE PADRE "THERE IS ENOUGH TO FEED YOUR CHURCH FOR 50 YEARS". THE TUNNEL/CAVE WAS OPEN AND ON A STEEP SLOPE FACING THE CHURCH.

13. THE DEVIL'S TRAIL OF TREASURE

CAMINO DEL DIABLO — THE OLD SONORA TRAIL FROM SONORA TO YUMA, ARIZONA, IS ABOUT 115 LEAGUES (250 MILES) AND THIS TRAIL WAS TRAVELED EXTENSIVELY. LITTLE OR NO WATER WAS AVAILABLE, ONLY AT YUMA AND CARRIZO SPRING 100 MILES ALONG THE TRAIL AND FROM TINAJAS ATLAS TO SONDITA, 150 MILES, WERE ONLY "TINAJAS" (MOUNTAIN WATER TANKS). ALONG THIS TRAIL TODAY CAN BE FOUND MANY THOUSANDS OF TREASURE ARTIFACTS IN THE FORM OF WAGON WHEELS, TRUNKS, WEAPONS, ITEMS BURIED TO EASE THE LOAD WHEN HORSES AND MULES DIED, WITH THE THOUGHT TO RETURN ONE DAY AND RECOVER. GOLD COINS AND FULL JEWELRY BOXES HAVE BEEN FOUND NEAR THE TRAIL. TAKE WATER, A METAL DETECTOR, WATER, WATER, AND A BIG TRUCK TO BRING BACK YOUR TREASURES. REMEMBER, ARTIFACTS **ARE** TREASURES AND MANY TIMES WORTH MORE THAN GOLD. THIS TRAIL IS A COIN-SHOOTERS PARADISE. (SEE TRAIL MAP ON PAGE 2.)

14. GOLD BARS AND COINS

A GREAT HIDDEN TREASURE OF GOLD BARS AND A VERY RICH SILVER MINE IS STILL UNFOUND NEAR THE TOWN OF ALAMOS, RANCHO SANTA BARBARA AT THE BASE OF GUADALUPE MOUNTAIN RANGE IN SONORA. DON FELIPE'S HACIENDA WAS ALONGSIDE THE MAYO RIVER WHICH CONTINUES TO FLOW THROUGH MAYO VALLEY AND ON TO THE SEA. THREE DAYS A WEEK MANY PACK HORSES TOOK SMELTED SILVER AND GOLD BARS TO SANTA BARBARA FROM THE DON'S HACIENDA (GOLD) AND MINES (SILVER). HIS SILVER MINES WERE IN GUADALUPE MOUNTAIN AND HIS GOLD MINES WERE IN SOBIA TO THE WEST. DON FELIPE WAS KILLED IN 1811 AND HIS REMAINING FAMILY MOVED TO MEXICO CITY. HIS GOLD MINES IN SOBIA HAVE NEVER BEEN FOUND AND HIS DAUGHTER "CLOTHILDE" YEARS LATER GAVE A CRUDE MAP TO HER SON STATING THAT HIS GRANDFATHER HAD HIDDEN MANY GOLD BARS AND COINS FOR CATTLE BUYING AND EMERGENCIES UNDER A HUGE TREE 250

VARAS FROM THEIR HACIENDA DIRECTLY OUT FROM HER FATHER'S BEDROOM WINDOW. BOTH TREASURE AND MINES REMAIN UNFOUND. THE GRANDSON NEVER NEEDED ANY MONEY AND NEVER LOOKED FOR THE HIDDEN TREASURE OR MINES. DON FELIPE'S MAP AND LETTER SURFACED IN THE EARLY 1900's IN THE HANDS OF A TREASURE HUNTER, BUT HE COULD NOT RELOCATE THE DON'S OLD HACIENDA LOCATION...CAN YOU?

15. ARMOUR, IDOLS AND AZTEC TREASURE CAVERN

ADJOINING THE SANTA CLARA RIO, WEST OF SAN JOSE DELA CRUZ IS A CAVE WITH A NARROW ENTRANCE THAT GOES DEEP INTO THE MOUNTAIN AND BECOMES A LARGE ROOM FULL OF GOLD AND SILVER BARS, OLD SPANISH ARMOUR, TRUNKS OF JEWELS AND FOREIGN GOLD ARTIFACTS AND TWO LARGE (18 INCH) GOLDEN IDOLS. AN OLD MEXICAN MAN FOUND THIS TREASURE BY ACCIDENT AND WAS ABLE TO SEE THE TREASURES BECAUSE OF 3 TO 4 AIR/SMOKE HOLES IN THE CEILING AND A SMALL FIRE HE STARTED IN THE ROOM. HE TOOK A FEW ITEMS AND IN DEPARTING CLOSED THE ENTRANCE AND MARKED IT WITH 3 DEAD BRANCHES OR LOGS. HE THEN WENT TO THE DIRECTOR OF THE NATIONAL MUSEUM OF MEXICO AND ASKED TO LEAD THE DIRECTOR TO THE TREASURE IN RETURN FOR A SMALL REWARD. THE DIRECTOR SAID THE ITEMS BROUGHT OUT WERE AZTEC BUT IF THERE WAS ARMOUR IN THE CAVERN IT WAS PROBABLY TREASURE HIDDEN BY THE CONQUISTADORES. THE DIRECTOR'S WIFE WAS QUITE ILL SO HE ASKED THE OLD MAN TO WAIT 2 WEEKS AND THEY WOULD GO, GIVING THE DIRECTOR TIME ALSO TO FORM AN OFFICIAL EXPEDITION TO THE NORTHWEST LOCATION. THE OLD MAN HAD A SEIZURE AND DID NOT LIVE LONG ENOUGH TO LEAD OR GO, SO IN 1956 THE DIRECTOR LED THE OFFICIAL GROUP WITH SOME SOLDIERS TO SEARCH THE SLOPES OF SANTA CLARA FOR THE CAVE. THEY SPENT OVER TWO WEEKS, BUT THEY DID NOT HAVE METAL DETECTORS OR ANY OTHER TYPE OF EQUIPMENT THAT WOULD HELP THEM. WITH THE EQUIPMENT AVAILABLE TODAY IT COULD BE FOUND A LOT EASIER THAN WINNING THE LOTTERY. THE

ONLY OTHER CLUE GIVEN BY THE OLD MEXICAN WAS THAT "DIRECTLY DOWN SLOPE FROM THE ENTRANCE, ABOUT 200 VARAS IS THE CANYON WASH AND IT WIDENED OUT ON BOTH SIDES LIKE A BIG SWIMMING POOL WITH A SMALL ISLAND NEAR THE MIDDLE ABOUT TEN VARAS SQUARE" — WHEN YOU FIND IT, SHIP ME ONE OF THE IDOLS — I REALLY LIKE THIS ONE.

16. MESA TREASURE

A GREAT TREASURE OF GOLD, SILVER AND JEWELS IS BURIED IN NORTHERN SONORA, EAST OF "CANENEA" NEAR THE BORDER AND AJO MOUNTAINS. THE TREASURE WAS PLACED IN A CAVE ON THE EAST SIDE OF A SMALL **FLAT TOPPED HILL**. ABOUT 65 MILES SOUTH EAST OF NOGALES, MEXICO.

17. TREASURES OF THE LOST MISSION

THE LOST MISSION OF SANTA ISABEL WAS BUILT FAR FROM ANY MINING ACTIVITIES AND FAR FROM ANY POPULATION. THIS MISSION IS DUE EAST OF SAN AGUSTIN, A 3 DAY WALK (APPROXIMATELY 96 MILES). THREE VERY WEALTHY MINE OWNERS JOINED FORCES TO HIDE MUCH OF THEIR TREASURES FROM THE GOVERNMENT AND TAXATION, ETC. THEY DECIDED TO BUILD A SMALL MISSION IN THIS ISOLATED AREA AS THE LANDMARK FOR THEIR HIDING PLACE. EACH OF THE 3 MINE OWNERS DUG SEPARATE MAJOR CAVES FOR THEIR TREASURES. THEY FOUND A PADRE TO BE IN CHARGE OF THE MISSION'S CONSTRUCTION — THUS, THERE WOULD BE NO SUSPICION OF MATERIALS BEING TRANSPORTED TO THE NEW MISSION AND TREASURES COULD BE HIDDEN IN THE CARGO TAKEN THERE TO LATER BE PLACED IN THE NEARBY CAVES. THE MISSION IS AT THE BASE OF A VERTICAL CLIFF ON THE RIDGE OF A NARROW CANYON ABOVE A YEAR-ROUND SPRING THAT FEEDS A SMALL LAKE. THE LAKE WAS SURROUNDED BY TOBACCO AND ARROWSEED PLANTS. THE PEAK OF SAN JUAN DE DIOS COULD BE SEEN FROM THE MISSION'S RIDGELINE...UNFOUND.

18. THE MOUNTAIN OF GOLD BEANS

THE LITTLE TOWN OF CAMOA ON THE MAYO RIVER, SONORA, HAD A MISSION THAT WAS THE BENEFICIARY OF A NEARBY MINE THAT POURED OUT BEAN SIZED GOLD NUGGETS. CONVERTED MAYO INDIANS POINTED OUT THE LOCATION OF THESE GOLD BEANS TO THE MISSION'S PADRE, WHO THEN DEVELOPED A TUNNEL MINE THAT HE HAD WORKED SPARINGLY AS MONEY WAS NEEDED. THE PADRE HAD THE MINE ENTRANCE CLOSED AFTER ABOUT TWO MONTHS OF WORK EACH YEAR OR TWO, AND THEN REOPENED AGAIN AS DESIRED. THIS LITTLE TOWN OF CAMOA WAS OVERRUN BY AN INDIAN UPRISING SHORTLY AFTER THE PADRE WAS ARRESTED AND SENT OUT OF MEXICO. CAMOA REMAINED UNINHABITED UNTIL THE 1850's AND DURING THE REBUILDING OF THE TOWN AND DIGGING UNDER THE OLD MISSION A RECTANGULAR CLAY BOX, MUCH LIKE A CHILD'S COFFIN, WAS FOUND WITH A GOLD CROWN AND A GOLD DAGGER AND AN OLD DOCUMENT THAT HAD STAINED AND ROTTED. HOWEVER, WHAT COULD BE READ SAID, "I STAND AT THE SHRINE'S MAIN DOOR AND LOOK **SOUTHEASTERLY** TO THE LARGE MOUNTAIN AND SEE THE LEDGE THAT HOLDS THE TUNNEL THAT POURS OUT THE GOLDEN BEANS IN GREAT QUANTITIES." THERE IS A MOUNTAIN NEARBY THAT THE INDIANS CALLED "ORO MANI", BUT MANY FEEL THAT THIS IS **NOT** THE CORRECT MOUNTAIN. LOOK FOR A PROMINENT LEDGE.

19. TIBURON (SHARK) ISLAND TREASURES

THE WATERS SURROUNDING TIBURON ISLAND IS HOME TO FEROCIOUS AND NUMEROUS SHARKS; HOWEVER, THE SERI INDIANS THAT OCCUPIED THE ISLAND ITSELF UNTIL THE EARLY 1900's WERE FAR MORE FEARED. THE SERIS WERE CANNIBALS, TOTALLY POSSESSIVE OF THEIR ISLAND, AND KILLED ISLAND INTRUDERS WITH POISONED DARTS, ARROWS AND SPEARS GLEANED FROM THE HUNDREDS OF THOUSANDS OF VENOMOUS SNAKES ON THIS 14 BY 28 MILE LONG ISLAND THAT LAY CLOSE TO THE EAST SHORE OF THE GULF OF CALIFORNIA. THE

INTERIOR IS HIGH AND RUGGED WITH FEW SPRINGS AND VERY HEAVY PALMETTO BRUSH. MEXICO'S FEDERAL TROOPS "INVADED" TIBURON FOUR TIMES ENDEAVORING TO REMOVE THE SERIS AND RE-ESTABLISH THEM ON THE MAINLAND WHERE THEY COULD BE "CONTROLLED". THE FOURTH TIME THEY WERE SUCCESSFUL AND THE SERI VILLAGES ARE NOW ON THE MAINLAND ABOUT 20 MILES AWAY AND A LIGHTHOUSE AND TWO FEDERAL GUARD STATIONS ARE ON THE ISLAND. MANY, MANY TREASURES ARE **WELL DOCUMENTED** TO HAVE BEEN BURIED ON TIBURON BY PIRATES, FRENCH SHIPS AND ENGLISH SHIPS, AS WELL AS MANY SAYING THAT AZTEC TREASURE AND SERI TREASURES ARE ALSO HIDDEN ON THE ISLAND. RICH GOLD ORE BODIES WERE LOCATED LESS THAN 6 FEET BELOW THE SURFACE BY ENGLISH EXPLORERS/GEOLOGISTS. LIEUTENANT C. ROVINSON OF ENGLAND PLUS OTHERS IN HIS GROUP WERE KILLED ON THE BEACH WHILE LOADING SOME OF THEIR RECOVERED TREASURES FROM THE ISLAND. AMERICAN SHIP CAPTAIN G. PORTER OF THE SHIP "WORLD" WAS KILLED ALONG WITH TWO CREW MEMBERS IN 1907 WHO WERE NAILED TO TREES ALONG THE BEACH. PROFESSOR H.E. MILLER, SUPERINTENDENT OF THE SCHOOLS OF ARIZONA, ALONG WITH CAPTAIN GUS ORLANDER OF THE SHIP "ELIZA", WHILE ENDEAVORING TO LOCATE A PITCHBLEND DEPOSIT ON TIBURON, WERE KILLED — THIS WAS LONG AFTER THE SERIS WERE BANNED FROM THE ISLAND — ARE THE SERIS STILL GUARDING THEIR NEARBY HOMELAND? TIBURON IS EASY OF ACCESS BY BOAT AND A DEEP METAL DETECTOR COULD MAKE YOU A "BILLIONAIRE" REAL QUICK. I'M NOT SURE THE GAMBLE IS WORTH IT.

20. MESA OF THE BULLS AZTEC TREASURE

THREE TO FOUR TONS OF GOLD AND SILVER OBJECTS AND ORNAMENTS WERE HIDDEN BY AZTECS BELOW THE "MESA OF THE BULLS" WHICH IS ABOUT 14 WALKING LEAGUES (30 MILES) FROM CHOIX ON THE CHOIX RIVER. ALL OF THE VILLAGE'S TREASURES WERE ORDERED TO BE PLACED IN THE "CUEVA PINTADA" (PAINTED CAVE), WHICH IS LOCATED, ACCORDING TO

REPORTS, A SHORT DISTANCE UP THE WEST BANK OF THE ARROYO DEL TORO CANYON WASH. THE CHIEF OF THE AZTEC VILLAGE WAS ADVISED OF THE APPROACHING SPANIARDS AND ISSUED THE FOLLOWING ORDER RECORDED BY "ESTEVAN": I WILL STAND TOMORROW MORNING WITH MY BACK TO THE TORO AND WHEN MY SHADOW FALLS ON THE PAINTED CAVE ON THE OPPOSITE SIDE OF THE CANYON ALL OF OUR TREASURES MUST BE WITHIN THIS CAVE AND IT WILL BE SEALED. THIS TREASURE CAVE HAS NEVER BEEN FOUND; HOWEVER, EVEN TODAY AFTER HEAVY ARROYO FLOODS SMALL GOLD AND SILVER ITEMS AND ORNAMENTS ARE FOUND IN THE WASH.

21. BEACHES OF GOLD AND JEWELRY

THERE ARE MANY BEACH AREAS IN MEXICO THAT HAVE ANNUALLY GIVEN UP TREASURES FOR HUNDREDS OF YEARS, USUALLY TO PEOPLE WITH METAL DETECTORS OR AFTER STORMS TO PEOPLE WITH "EAGLE EYES". SOME OF THE "BEACHES" ARE ONLY A FEW FEET WIDE AT LOW TIDE AND DIFFICULT TO REACH BUT WELL WORTH THE EFFORT.

ALONG THE **GULF OF MEXICO** COAST'S BEACHES, BOTH SPANISH AND AZTEC TREASURES ARE FOUND WASHED IN FROM SPANISH GALLEONS THAT WRECKED NEAR SHORE, MOSTLY FROM GREAT STORMS AND HURRICANES. IN THE 1960's A MAN WALKING KNEE DEEP IN THE WATER STUBBED HIS TOE ON A 62-POUND BAR OF SILVER. DURING THE NEXT SIX MONTHS HE FOUND OVER $300,000.00 OF TREASURE BY DRAGGING HIS FEET AROUND THAT AREA IN A FEW FEET OF WATER. THE BEACHES ALONG THE **GULF OF MEXICO** ARE THE RICHEST.

ALSO FOUND ALONG THE **PACIFIC OCEAN** AND HIGH IN **THE SEA OF CORTEZ/GULF OF CALIFORNIA** ARE TREASURES ON THE BEACH. THESE ARE FROM WRECKED MANILA GALLEONS, PIRATE SHIPS AND SOME POSSIBLY WERE BURIED TREASURES THAT UNCOVERED AND SPREAD OUT IN STORMS. MAINLY GOLD

DOUBLOONS, PIECES OF EIGHT AND RINGS ARE FOUND AT THESE **BAJA, CALIFORNIA, LOCATIONS.**

22. SPANISH/AZTEC TREASURE CAVES

IN 1948 A MAJOR AZTEC TREASURE WAS FOUND ABOUT 90 AIR MILES NORTHWEST OF MEXICO CITY IN THE MOUNTAINS 8 MILES SOUTH OF THE SMALL TOWN OF "TETELA". MANUEL RAMIRIZ HAD SPENT MOST OF HIS LIFE LOOKING FOR THIS AND TWO OTHER HIDDEN TREASURE CAVES NEARBY. MANUEL HAD BEEN GIVEN THREE MAPS MANY YEARS AGO BY HIS FATHER-IN-LAW WHO TOLD MANUEL THAT THREE CAVES ALL WITHIN A MILE OF EACH OTHER WERE FULL OF TREASURES HIDDEN BY BANDITS WHO ROBBED A CONVOY THAT WAS TAKING THE TREASURE TO VERA CRUZ FOR SHIPMENT TO SPAIN. IN 1948 MANUEL AND HIS FOUR SONS FOUND AND OPENED ONE OF THE CAVES — THE WORD GOT OUT AND THE MEXICAN GOVERNMENT STEPPED IN AND TOOK IT ALL. IT WAS IN THE NEWSPAPERS IN MEXICO CITY TELLING ABOUT THE "HUGE AZTEC TREASURE FIND" NEAR "TETELA" — AND THEN — NO MORE STORIES OR INFORMATION. IT SEEMS THAT THE GOVERNMENT DID NOT WANT TO TALK ABOUT IT — OR TELL WHAT THEY DID WITH THE TREASURE. ABOUT TWO YEARS LATER MANUEL WAS INTERVIEWED (HE AND HIS SONS HAD BEEN KEPT IN JAIL FOR SIX MONTHS) AND HE SAID THAT HIS OTHER TWO MAPS TO THE OTHER NEARBY TREASURE CAVES WERE MISSING — BUT THAT IT DIDN'T MATTER BECAUSE HE LEARNED THAT THEY WERE "NATIONAL" TREASURES AND IT WAS ILLEGAL FOR "INDIVIDUALS TO OWN NATIONAL TREASURES". MANY OF MEXICO'S LAWS HAVE CHANGED SINCE 1948 — MAYBE IT'S OK TO FIND AN AZTEC TREASURE NOW. IF SO, I'D SURE SEARCH A ONE-MILE RADIUS AROUND THE CAVE THAT MANUEL AND HIS SONS FOUND.

23. SKULL AND TREASURE CAVERN

ABOUT FIVE TO SIX MILES S.S.W. OF "COBA" IN THE JUNGLE IS A LOW SWAMPLIKE AREA OF 20 TO 30 ACRES IN SIZE AND ON THE

WEST BANK OF THIS LOW AREA RISES UP A "KNOB" OF ROCK ABOUT 15 FEET TALL, 60 FEET LONG AND 30 FEET WIDE **THAT LOOKS LIKE A LARGE LOAF OF BREAD**. MARTIN G. FARNSWORTH, A WEALTHY STUDENT (AT AGE 46) OF ARCHAEOLOGY FROM ENGLAND, WROTE THE FOLLOWING IN HIS TWO-YEAR DIARY OUTLINING HIS ACTIVITIES IN THE YUCATAN AND ENVIRONS. MARTIN DIED IN THE YUCATAN JUNGLE OF SOME TYPE OF ACCIDENTAL POISONING, HIS NATIVE GUIDES AND LABORERS REPORTED.

MARTIN'S NOTES REVEAL A FASCINATION OF THIS BREAD-SHAPED ROCK — IT LOOKED MAN-MADE BUT IT WASN'T. SOME EIGHT MONTHS BEFORE HE DIED, HIS DIARY STATES: "IN OUR PASSING MY LOAF OF BREAD TODAY I NOTICED THE TOP OF A POSSIBLE CAVE/TUNNEL ENTRANCE AT THE SWAMP WATER LEVEL. I POINTED IT OUT AND WE WILL CLEAR AND CHECK IT OUT FIRST OPPORTUNITY. TWO WEEKS LATER WITH THE HELP OF LOGS AND STAKES WE FOUND AND ENTERED A TUNNEL THAT OPENED INTO A MAJOR CAVERN WITH CARVED STEPS LEADING UP ABOVE GROUND LEVEL TO A LARGE ROOM WITH 11" WIDE X 14" HIGH NICHES CUT INTO ITS WALLS EACH WITH A SKULL FACING ME (MAYBE 250 OF THEM). SOME LIGHT COMES FROM 47 HOLES IN THE DOME OF THIS ROCK — EACH OF THE DIAMETER OF 4" TO 8". AT THE FAR BACK END IS A FLAT-FACED WALL ABOUT 10' HIGH BY 20' WIDE WITH COLORED DESIGNS AND PETROGLYPHS. THE FLAT FLOOR EXTENDING OUT BELOW THE MARKINGS IS FULL OF JARS, BOWLS, GOLD OBJECTS, TURQUOISE, KNIVES AND SILVER OBJECTS. TOOK 34 PHOTOS. I HAVE TAKEN THE SMALL GOLD ANIMAL AND GOLD AND JADE HANDLED KNIFE SHOWN IN THE FOREGROUND OF MY PHOTOS.

MY MEN ARE MOST UPSET AND WILL NOT TOUCH ANYTHING FOR IT IS ALL "PROTECTED" BY THE SKULLS (SPIRITS). WE REMOVED OUR LOG WALL AND STAKES — I WILL TAKE NO MORE ITEMS AT THIS TIME".

DIARY: 6 DAYS LATER — PHOTO OF ROOM SENT HOME (ENGLAND) FOR DEVELOPING.

NO MORE MENTION OF MARTIN'S GREAT FIND IS IN THE DIARY. THE PHOTOS NEVER REACHED HIS FAMILY IN ENGLAND BUT HIS DIARY DID. IT'S STILL UNFOUND — OR AT LEAST UNREPORTED.

24. SMALL MAYAN TEMPLE

IN 1981 THE M.A.G. (MAYAN ARCHAEOLOGICAL GROUP) OF FLORIDA, HEADED BY GENE HEARTMAN, LOCATED A SMALL MAYAN TEMPLE OR STRUCTURE JUST A FEW MILES SOUTH OF THE YUCATAN BORDER POINT IN QUINTANA ROO, SOUTHWEST OF PUERTO ARTURO. HEARTMAN REPORTED HIS FIND TO THE AUTHORITIES AND REQUESTED GUARDS AND OFFICIALS TO BE APPOINTED TO HIS PROJECT UPON HIS RETURN. HE SAID HE WAS GOING TO FLORIDA AND CALIFORNIA TO ENGAGE A FILM CREW TO DOCUMENT THEIR FIND.

UNFORTUNATELY, HEARTMAN WAS FOUND TO BE SMUGGLING BACK TO THE U.S. A GOLD HANDLED HATCHET, SIX 3-1/2-4-1/4" GOLD DISCS. THREE GOLD PINS IN THE SHAPE/DESIGN OF SNAKES AND ONE 8-1/4" BY 11-1/3" BY 1/2" THICK SOLID GOLD OBJECT WITH INSCRIPTIONS AND DESIGNS. SOMEHOW HE "BOUGHT" HIS WAY OUT OF MEXICO AND IS "PERSONA NON GRATA" — AND HIS FABULOUS SMALL TEMPLE REMAINS — UNFOUND.

25. UNDERGROUND RIVER WITH GOLD IDOLS

ABOUT 90 MILES EAST OF ACAPULCO AND 30 MILES NORTH ABOUT MID POINT BETWEEN QUETZALAPA AND IXCUINATOYAC IS THE END OF A RIDGELINE OF A MOUNTAIN RANGE THAT DROPS DOWN INTO A VALLEY, A LOW DESERT AREA. RIGHT THERE AT THE POINT OF THE DROP IS AN OPENING, LARGE AND IRREGULAR IN A SHAPE THAT EXTENDS DOWNWARD TO ABOUT THE LEVEL OF THE DESERT FLOOR. THIS WAS THE GENERAL

AREA WHERE RAMON CARED FOR HIS FAMILY'S SHEEP AND A FEW HEAD OF CATTLE. RAMON SAW THE LARGE OPENING ONE DAY AND TOLD HIS FATHER AND BROTHERS — "MAYBE IT'S A RICH OLD SPANISH MINE," HE SAID. WELL, HIS FATHER SUPERVISED AND HIS BOYS CLIMBED DOWN WITH TORCHES AND LANTERNS. IT KEPT GOING DOWN AND THEY FOUND LARGE "MESAS" ALONG THE WAY THAT HAD OLD FIREPLACES WITH COOKED BONES IN THEM. IT TOOK OVER A YEAR AND TEN TRIPS FOR THEM TO GET TO THE BOTTOM (A FOUR-HOUR CLIMB DOWN) WHERE THEY FOUND A SLOW MOVING, DEEP AND 25' TO 30' WIDE RIVER WITH A LARGE OPEN AREA ON THE OTHER SIDE OF THE RIVER. THEY THREW A TORCH AND THEY SEEMED TO SEE **OBJECTS** ON THE FLOOR. ONLY JESUS COULD SWIM AND HE WOULDN'T TRY IT. HIS FATHER CONVINCED HIM TO SWIM ACROSS AND SEE WHAT WAS THERE. ALSO THE FATHER BROUGHT BIG FLASHLIGHTS THAT SEEMED TO ILLUMINATE **GOLD OBJECTS** ON THE OTHER SIDE OF THE NARROW RIVER.

RAMON AND HIS BROTHERS BROUGHT OUT A NINE-POUND SOLID GOLD STATUE OF A BULL AND TWO TWO-POUND GOLD CUPS AND REPORTED THAT 100 TO 120 GOLD OBJECTS FROM 4" TO 10" HIGH WERE SITTING EVENLY SPACED ABOUT ONE VARA APART AND WERE ALL OVER THE FLOOR.

RAMON AND HIS SONS PLANNED A TEN-DAY TRIP TO REMOVE ALL ITEMS. THEY NEVER RETURNED FORM THE TRIP. RAMON'S WIFE AND MOTHER OF HIS SONS TOLD THE STORY TO A FRIEND AND GAVE HIM ONE OF THE GOLD CUPS TO LOOK FOR THEM BUT NEITHER THE ENTRANCE OR ANY OF THEIR EQUIPMENT WAS FOUND. ABOUT A YEAR LATER SHE WENT TO SAN MARCOS TO SEE HER COUSIN WHO TOOK HER TO THE LOCAL POLICE CHIEF. SHE SHOWED HIM THE GOLD BULL AND GAVE HIM THE OTHER GOLD CUP. "I KNOW THEY HAVE GONE TO GOD BUT I MUST HAVE THEM BURIED AND BLESSED PROPERLY," SHE SAID. "THIS CUP IS FOR YOU TO SEARCH FOR THEM. THIS GOLD BULL WILL BE YOUR PAYMENT WHEN YOU FIND THEM, PLUS ALL OF THE

TREASURE." THE POLICE CHIEF HIRED MEN TO SEARCH AND HE HIMSELF SEARCHED UNTIL HE DIED IN 1986 — STILL UNFOUND.

26. WELL, WELL, WELL, 5 MILLION?

ABOUT 20 MILES EAST OF "MONCLOVA" IS THE LITTLE TOWN OF "LAS CABRAS" AT THE FOOT OF A SMALL MOUNTAIN RANGE. MANY YEARS AGO A SMALL SPANISH HACIENDA WAS IN THE FOOTHILLS OF THESE MOUNTAINS AND OWNED BY DON ALPHONSUS DE MADRID. DON ALPHONSUS RETURNED TO SPAIN IN 1928 AT THE REQUEST (ORDER) OF MEXICO'S PRESIDENT AND HE DEPARTED RAPIDLY. FIVE YEARS LATER THE DON WROTE THE FOLLOWING LETTER TO THE PADRE AT THE CATHEDRAL OF MONCLOVA. THIS LETTER SURFACED IN THE CATHEDRAL'S OLD RECORD FILES IN THE MID 1980's.

JUNE 6, 1833

DEAR PADRE ERNESTO:

IT HAS BEEN MANY YEARS AND I PRAY YOU ARE WELL — ETC.

NEITHER I NOR MINE WILL BE RETURNING AS WE HAD HOPED AND PRAYED. THEREFORE, I HEREWITH GIFT TO YOU AND THE CHURCH ONE HALF OF MY POSSESSIONS LEFT AT MY HACIENDA. THE REMAINING HALF I ASK YOU TO LEAVE THERE JUST IN CASE I OR MINE SOMEDAY DO RETURN.

"YOU WILL RECALL THE GREAT WELL AT MY HACIENDA WHERE WE STOOD SHADED BY THE OVERHANGING TREE ON THE DAY YOU BAPTIZED MY SON MIGUEL. IT IS HERE, SIX VARAS BELOW THE RING AND ON THE WEST SIDE WALL THAT HIDES THE DOORWAY TO MY ROOM OF 5 MILLION IN GOLD."

WE DON'T KNOW IF THE PADRE EVER GOT HIS HALF — BUT, NO MATTER, THE OTHER HALF MAY STILL BE THERE — WAITING. (SEE PAGE 13.)

27. TREASURE SHELTER ROCKS

WAY BACK IN THE LATE 1400's PIRATES DEVISED CODES, SIGNS, SYMBOLS AND MONUMENTS FOR PRIVATE COMMUNICATIONS/MESSAGES TO BE USED THROUGHOUT THE WORLD. THE "ROCK SHELTER" SHOWN ON PAGE 15 WAS THE MONUMENT THAT THEY CONSTRUCTED ON AN **ISLAND** OR AT AN **INLET, BAY** OR **ALONG A COASTLINE** THAT GAVE THE MESSAGE "THIS IS AN AREA **PROTECTED FROM WEATHER — ANCHOR OR MOOR SHIP HERE"**. DOWN THE SLOPE OF "PUNTA MITA", THE NORTH POINT OF THE FAMOUS PUERTA VALLARTA'S BAY, STOOD ONE OF THESE TELLING ALL PIRATE SHIPS THAT IT WAS A SAFE/**WEATHER PROTECTED** HARBOR.

IN THE VERY EARLY 1600's, THE SPANISH LEARNED OF THIS MONUMENT AND ITS PIRATE MEANING AND BEGAN USING THIS MONUMENT IN **INLAND LOCATIONS** TO FREQUENTLY **BURY/HIDE TREASURES UNDER THIS MONUMENT ROCK**. ONE SUCH "TREASURE SHELTER BOULDER" WAS REMOVED DURING THE GRADING AND CLEARING OF A COASTAL POINT OF LAND NEAR MIAMI, FLORIDA, FOR THE CONSTRUCTION OF A HOTEL IN 1938. AN ESTIMATED 11 MILLION DOLLARS WAS UNEARTHED UNDER THE CENTER OF THIS BOULDER HAVING BEEN HIDDEN BY SPANISH, THE NEWSPAPERS REPORTED. HOWEVER, PIRATES WERE MORE LIKELY TO HAVE HIDDEN THESE TREASURES.

BE ALERT TO THESE CARVED/CUT SHELTER MONUMENTS WHEREVER THEY MAY BE FOUND. TREASURES AND/OR A MINE ENTRANCE MAY WELL BE **UNDER THIS BOULDER** THAT IS CARVED IN SUCH A MANNER THAT USUALLY FOUR TO SIX PEOPLE CAN STAND INSIDE THE HOLLOWED AREA AND BE PROTECTED FROM RAIN.

28. TREASURE BURIAL MOUNDS

A NATIVE INDIAN BOY ABOUT 16 YEARS OLD TOLD A GROUP OF GERMAN ARCHAEOLOGISTS IN 1987 THAT WHEN HE WAS ABOUT

EIGHT YEARS OLD HE WENT WITH HIS FATHER IN THE JUNGLE A LITTLE WEST OF "BECANCHEN" (ABOUT 90 MILES DUE EAST OF "CAMPECHE") AND THEY SPOTTED A SMALL DEER ON A RIDGELINE ABOUT 40 FEET ABOVE THEM. THE DEER WAS WIGGLING ABOUT BUT DID NOT RUN AWAY SO FATHER AND SON CLIMBED UP TO THE DEER. "WE FOUND THAT THE DEER HAD ONE OF HIS LEGS STUCK DOWN INTO THE GROUND RIGHT UP AGAINST A LARGE FLAT 600 TO 800 POUND ROCK LYING ON THE RIDGELINE. WE KILLED THE DEER AND PULLED HIS LEG OUT OF THE GROUND. MY FATHER LOOKED DOWN THE HOLE AND PUT A LONG STICK DOWN THE HOLE. THEN WE DUG DOWN AND UNDER A BIT AND DROPPED STONES THAT TOLD US THAT IT WAS DEEP AND HARD AT THE BOTTOM. WE WENT BACK WITH ROPES, FLASHLIGHTS AND SHOVELS AND DUG BUT HIT HARD ROCK SO WE ANGLED THE HOLE UNDER THE BIG FLAT ROCK AND I WAS ABLE TO GET MY HEAD AND ARM WITH A FLASHLIGHT IN SO THAT I COULD LOOK DOWN. THERE WERE BODIES LYING FLAT ON LARGE FLAT ROCKS, BOWLS, OBJECTS SITTING ON LITTLE ROCK STANDS AND LOTS OF GOLD THINGS — I'M SURE. WE HAD NO TOOLS TO BREAK THE ROCK OR ENLARGE THE HOLE SO THAT MY FATHER COULD SEE IN. THAT NIGHT WE COVERED OUR HOLE WITH A BIG ROCK AND DIRT AND LEFT FOR HOME. MY FATHER FELL ON THE TRIP BACK AND CUT HIS LEG BADLY. WE LEFT THE DEER MEAT THERE AND HID OUR TOOLS NEARBY. IT TOOK US TWO DAYS TO GET HOME AND FATHER'S LEG SWELLED WITH POISON. FATHER DIED AT HOME TEN DAYS LATER. MOTHER SAID, 'NEVER GO BACK THERE. THE SPIRITS KILLED YOUR FATHER'. I'M SURE I CAN TAKE YOU THERE IF YOU PAY ME", THE BOY TOLD THE GERMANS. HE TRIED TO LEAD THEM BUT COULD NOT FIND THE LOW RIDGELINE WITH THE LARGE FLAT ROCK THAT COVERED THE ENTRANCE OR COVERED SMOKE HOLE — STILL UNFOUND.

Other Books By the Author:

"Treasure-Signs, Symbols, Shadows and Sun Signs"

©TX-3-225535
ISBN 0-932156-0-4

"Spanish Monuments & Trailmakers to Treasure"

©TX-577402
ISBN 0-9632156-1-2

"Death Traps to Treasure"

©TXu652-300
ISBN 0-9632156-2-0

This one

"Unfound Treasures of Mexico"

(Español & English)
ISBN 0-9632156-4-7

Next Up

"Treasure Secrets of the Lost Dutchman"

ISBN 0-9632156-3-9

Contenido

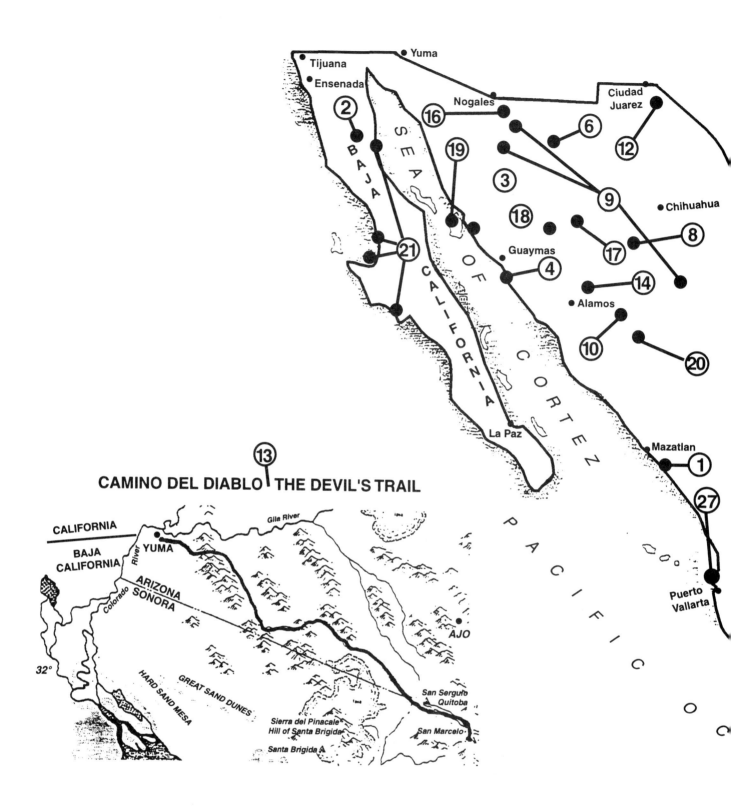

CAMINO DEL DIABLO THE DEVIL'S TRAIL

Tesoros No Encontrado
En Mexico "Carlos"

Unfound Treasures
of Mexico

© Charles A. Kenworthy

DEDICADO A MIS AMIGOS DE MUCHOS ANOS, MEJICANOS, LATINOS Y ESPAÑOLES QUE A TANIDO EL PLACER DE TRABAJAR EN BUSCA Y RECUPERACION DE TESOROS A REDONDO EL MUNDO. INCLUIDO LOS ARCHIVOS Y SUB-ARCHIVOS DE MEXICO, Y LOS MIEMBROS PERSONALES DEL MUSEO. NACIONAL DE ANTROPOLOGIA Y LOS SUB-ARCHIVOS DEL LOS ARCHIVOS DE ESPAÑA. EN ADICION QUIERO DEDICAR ESTE LIBRO A LAS DOS FAMILAS MEJICANAS QUE ME PRESTARON SU MAPAS ANTIGUS EN CODIGO DE TESORO ESPAÑOLAS/MEJICANOS. LAS FAMILAS NO ENTIENDEN LAS MAPAS, PERO JUNTOS OBTENIMOS EXITO EN DOS TESOROS EN ARIZONA, Y ANDAMOS CERCA DE OTRO TESORO EN CALIFORNIA.

UN "GRAN AGRADECIMENTO" PARA CATARINO CASTRO, LALO TRETO, JESUS ROJAS, JUAN PERALTA, MARIA Y RiCARDO GONZALES POR SU AYUDA EN EL PASADO, Y POR EL PRESENTE EN DECUBRIR ESAS OLLAS DE ORO EN LOS EXTREMOS DEL ARCO IRIS.

TAMBIEN CON GRACIAS ESPECIAL PARA EL CASADOR DE TESOROS Y TRADUCRO DESTE LIBRO, GILBERTO TRUJILLO DE APACHE JUNCTION, ARIZONA.

EN TODO EL MUNDO YO CONSIDERO MEJICO NO MAS SECRDARIO A PERU EN LAS REGIONES DE TESOROS PERDIDOS Y PERDIDAS/ESCONDIDAS MINAS DE ENORME VALOR.

MEJICOS INMENSO TESOROS PERDIDOS COMENZAN CON LOS TESOROS ESCONDIDOS DE LOS MAYAS Y LOS AZTECAS.

EN SEQUIDA LOS AÑOS DE 1810 A 1821 EN LA EPOCA DE LA REVOLUCION, CUANDO EL PADRE MIGUEL HIDALGO JUNTO LOS INDIOS, PEONES, LOS ESCLAVOS Y LOS MEJICANOS AL LA REVUELTA CONTRA EL DOMINIO DE ESPAÑA, UNA PERIODA DE ONCE ANOS DONDE LOS MEJICANOS GANARON INDEPENDENCIA DE ESPAÑA. DURANTE ESTOS ONCE ANOS DE COÑBATE, ESPAÑA FUE FUERZADA A LLAMAR LOS SOLDADOS DE LAS AREAS DEL NORTE DONDE ESTAVAN DANDO PROTECCION A MAS QUE CIEN MINAS, VECINDARIOS Y MISIONS. MAS QUE MIL TESOROS GRANDES Y PEQUEÑOS Y MINAS TAMBIEN ESCONDIERON LOS MINEROS, DUENOS DE MINAS, FAMILAS, SOLDADOS Y MISONAS CON LA INTENSION DE VOLVER ALGUN DIA A RECUPERAR LO QUE ESCONDIERON PERO NUNCA VOLVERON PORQUE ESPAÑA PERDIO LA GUERRA Y MEJICO GANO SU INDEPENDENCIA.

ENTONCES ENTRE 1821 Y 1847 MEJICO TUVO MUCHAS REVOLCIONAS Y MAS QUE VEINTE PRESIDENTES Y GOBIERNOS. EN 1848 MEJICO PERDIO MUCHAS TIERRAS EN EL NORTE A LOS ESTADOS UNIDOS. CON ESTE CONSTANTE CONFUSION FUE IMPOSIBLE ORGANIZAR UN ESFUERZO PARA ENCONTRAR LOS TESOROS PERDIDOS Y LAS MINAS ESCONDIDAS. POR MAYORIA MAS DE TODOS LOS TESOROS Y MINAS ESTAN PERDIDAS TODAVIA POR ESTOS MUCHOS AÑOS.

NOSTROS SEMOS AFORTUNADOS QUE ENCONTRAMOS DOS TESOROS EN MEJICO, PERO LOS DOS TESOROS ESTABAN MENOS QUE OCHENTA MIAS AL SUR DE LAS FRONTERA. ESTABA PREOCUPADO A BUSCAR TESOROS MAS PARA EL SUR PORQUE LOS DERECHOS DE MEJICO ERAN MUY RIGOROSOS. HORA

ENTIENDO QUE ES MAS FACILE PARA CONSEQUIR PERMISOS PARA BUSCAR TESOROS — SI APLICAN.

LA MEJOR ESPERANZA QUE UN CAZADOR DE TESOROS PUEDE ENCONTRAR ES QUE SU INFORMACION ESTA CORRECTA Y EXACTA Y QUE SU MINA/TESORO EN VERDA EXISTO EN UN TIEMPO. PERO EL UNICO FACTOR ES SI ALGUIEN LO DESCUBRIO Y SE ESTA QUITEO Y SILENCIO CON EL TESORO.

EN SEGUNDO, LO MAS IMPORTANTE FACTOR DEL CAZADOR ES CONOCIMIENTO/COMPRENSION DE SEÑAS, SIMBOLOS, MARCAS EN SENDEROS, SEÑAS EN SENDEROS Y CODIGOS EN MAPAS Y EN EL CAMPO. ESCRITORES DE "CUENTOS" DE TESOROS AN CON-FUNDIDO CON ERROR A LOS CAZADORES DE TESORO POR MUCHOS AÑOS. AL COPIAR UNOS ESCRITORES EN INVESTIGATION INTERPRETARON CON ERROR LAS SEÑAS. POR EJEMPLO "EL TESORO ESTA ESCONDIDO EN UNA MINA CUBRIDA DOS LIGAS AL SUR OESTE DE "X". EL ESCRITOR EN SEGUIDA NOS DICE QUE UNA LIGA ERA ENTRE TRES Y TRES Y MEDIO MIAS EN DISTANCIA. ESTO ES VERDA PARA UNA LIGA NAVAL PERO NO PARA UNA LIGA EN TIERRA. UNA LIGA EN TIERRA ERA 2.18 MIAS. SIN EMBARGO MUCHOS CAZADORES PEREIRON ANOS BUSCANDO EN REGIONES PASADAS DEL LAS ZONAS DE INTERES — POR LA CULPA DE ESTOS ESCRITORES.

COMIENZANDO EN 1974 YO COMMENCE A PONER ME EN CONTACTO DIRECTAMENTE Y INDIRECTAMENTE CON LOS ARCHIVOS Y SUB-ARCHIVOS DE FRANCIA, ESPAÑA Y LA VATICA. PERO LOS ARCHIVOS DE LA CUIDAD DE MEJICO ERAN "MANOS A FUERA", PERO ARREGLOS CON UN MINISTRO NAVAL NOS POÑEO EN UN BUEN CONTACTO. COMIENZANDO EN 1978 COMMENCE A RECIBER NOTICIAS DE DESCUBRIMIENTOS DE VARIOS ARCHIVOS. SIN VER LA INFORMACION ME COMMENCE ADIVINAR LOS VALORES Y LE DI PRECIO A LAS COPIAS. AMOS RECIBIDO MUCHAS COPIAS DE TESOROS ESCONDIDOS Y DE MINAS EM FORMA DE MAPAS Y DOCUMENTOS ESCRITOS A MANO.

DESGRACIADAMENTE LA MAYORIA NO ENSEÑAN EL ESTADO, ZONA, O PAIS PARA LOCALIZAR EL PUNTO EN UNA MAPA.

EN 1983 ME LLEGO UNA CARTA DECLARANDO QUE SE ENCONTRARON 116 PAGINAS DEL REY DE ESPAÑA CON REGLAS Y REGULACIONS PARA MINAS Y EXPLORACION EN EL MUNDO NUEVO. INCLUIDO ERAN 34 PAGINAS DE SEÑALES EN CODIGO Y SIMBOLOS TAMBIEN PARA USO EN DOCUMENTOS Y MAPAS Y SUS INTERPRETACIONS: TAMBIEN INCLUIDOS ESTABAN DIBUJOS EN MARCAS EN SENDEROS Y EN MONUMENTOS QUE ESPAÑA POR LEY ORDENO CONSTRUIR, "ABAJO PENA DE ESPAÑA" EN SEQUIDA DE TODOS SENDEROS DE TESORO/MINAS.

PARA LOS ULTIMOS DE LOS 1500's, NUEVO MEJICO ESTUVO COLONIZADO POR LOS ESPAÑOLES CON SU PRIMERO GOBER-NADOR JUAN DE ONATE. ONATE ESTABLECIO SAN GABRIEL COMO EL PRIMER CAPITAL DE NUEVO MEJICO, PERO NUNCA PROSPERO. ESPAÑA REEMPLAZO A ONATE CON PEDRO DE PERALTA QUE DEJO SANTA FE COMO LA CAPITAL. AQUI EN SANTA FE FUE QUE EL PALACIO DE GOBERNADORES SE CUMPLIO EN 1609. ESTE PALACIO ERA PARA GOBERNARE MEJICO EN EL NORTE. EN SEQUIDA DEL PALACIO DE GOBERBNADORES EL CATEDRAL DE SAN MIGUEL ESTUVO CONSTRUIDO Y EN OPERACION EN 1636.

ESTE ERA EL PUNTO CENTRAL PARA LA IGLESIA PARA CONVERTIR ALMAS Y TAMBIEN PARA ALLUDAR CON LAS PROBLEMAS EN EL PALACIO DE GOBERNADORES. PARECE QUE LOS MINEROS CRISTIANOS SE ENCONTRAVAN EN REBELION SI NO ESTABA UN PADRE PARA DAR LA ULTIMA CONFESION O LA ULTIMA ORACION EN LAS MINAS CON MUCHO DISTANCIA, (SE ENCONTRABAN MUCHAS MUERTES). ASI LA SOLUCION ERA BUENA PARA ESPAÑA Y LA IGLESIA TAMBIEN.

LA IGLESIA PODIA EXTENDER SU PALABRA EN DISTANCIAS NUEVAS CON EXPLORACION DE NUEVAS MINAS HECHAS POR ESPAÑA, Y EL "HOMBRE RELIGIOSO" DABA "CALMA Y CONFIANZA" AL GRUPO DE MINEROS/EXPLORADORES QUE

ESTABAN EN REVUETA MAS Y MAS SEQUIDO. EN ESTA MANERA DE COOPERACION LA IGLESIA Y ESPAÑA TRABAJAN MANO A MANO PARA COMPLETAR SUS DIFERENTES ASUNTOS.

EL PALACIO EN SANTA FE ERA EL CUARTEL GENERAL DE ESPAÑA PARA COMPLIR LAS LEYES DEL REY, POR EL NORTE DE MEJICO INCLUIDO, CALIFORNIA, TEXAS, ARIZONA, COLORADO, UTAH, NUEVO, MEXICO, NEVADA, LOUISIANA, KENTUCKY, ETC. LA MAYOR PARTE DE MEJICO EN ESTE TEIMPO ESTABA GOVERNADA POR LA CUIDAD DE MEJICO. LAS ACTIVIDADES DE EXPLORATION Y MINERA ERAN LOS PRIMEROS DEBERAS DEL PALACIO. LA COLECCION DE LAS HACIENDAS, MINEROS Y LOS RELIGIOSOS EL 15 A 20% PARA EL REY Y EL TRANSPORTE DE TESOROS PARA ESPAÑA, Y ENSENANADO A CADA HACIENDA LOS CODIS Y SIMBOLOS QUE ERAN PARA USAR EN MAPAS DE TESOROS, EN MONUMENTOS Y COMO USAR LOS, Y TAMBIEN COMO CONSTRUIR LOS CODES Y SIMBOLOS EN LOS CAMINOS PARA LAS MINAS Y TESOROS. ELLOS ENSEÑA VAN DOS PASEANTES CON BRUJULAS Y PERSONAS DE MAPAS PARA CADA HACIENDA. DESPUES DE ESTABLECER LA MAINAS LES DABAN DOS SUPERVISORS DE MONUMENTOS PARA MARCAR RASTROS. DESPUES CUANDO EL PALACIO RECIBIA LAS MAPAS DE TESOROS Y MINAS, MANDAVAN UN GRUPO PARA LA HACIENDA PARA SEGUIR CON LAS MAPAS LOS CAMINOS PARA LAS MINAS, Y DESPUES INFORMAR AL PALACIO EL PRECISO DE LAS MONUMENTOS MARCOS Y LOS CODIS DE LAS MAPAS DE TESOROS, ENTONCES EL PALACIO MANDAVA PARA ESPAÑA COPIAS DEL LAS MAPAS PARA EL REY DE ESPAÑA, Y PARA EL PALACIO EN LA CUIDAD DE MEJICO, Y UNA COPIA PARA EL PALACIO DE SANTA FE. LAS MAPAS ERAN PARA ASEGUARAR SE UN DESASTRE SUCEDIA A LOS MINEROS O LAS HACIENDAS, ESPAÑA PODIA HALLAR LAS A MINAS Y LOS TESOROS, Y NO PERDER LOS POR CIENTOS.

LOS ARCHIVOS EN ROMA (VATICAN) POSIBLE CONTEÑEN MAS DOCUMENTOS QUE ESPAÑA TIENE DE LA EXPLORACION ACTIVIDAD EN MINERA, EN EL NUEVO MUNDO POR ESTA RAZON: 1. LOS ARCHIVOS DE ESPAÑA TUVIERON UNOS DESASTRES DE

DILUVIOS Y FUEGOS. 2. LAS FILAS DE ESPAÑA NUNCA ESTABAN ORGANIZADAS POR EJEMPLO: BULTOS DE DOCUMENTOS DE 1682 HASTA 1685 TIENEN CARTAS DEL MEDIO DE 1700's. 3. "LOS RELIGIOSOS," DESIGNADOS PARA LOS GRUPOS DE MINERA, Y POR CIERTO ERAN LOS MAS EDUCADOS DE LOS GRUPOS, Y ERAN LOS CREADORES DE MAPAS CONCODIS, OR ERAN AYUDANTES, PERO CUALQUIER MODO COPIAS ENCONTRAN EL CAMINO PARA ROMA. POCA INFORMACION SE ENCONTRA POR LOS JESUITS, PORQUE EN ESOS DIAS LA INFORMACION ERA NO MAS PARA LA "SOCIEDAD" (LA SOCIEDAD DE JESUS "S.J."). LAS FILAS EN SUS ARCHIVOS ERAN IMPOSIBLE A OBTENER. LAS MAPAS ESTAN LLENAS DE SEÑAS, SIMBOLOS, Y SIBOLISMO RELIGIOSO CON BUENA RAZON. NO MAS DOS COSAS ESTABAN "PASANDO" EN ESTE MUNDO NUEVO MINERA/EXPLORATION Y "RELIGION".

TODOS LOS ESPANOLES Y MEJICANOS Y LOS "RELIGIOSOS" HACEN LA LUCHA DE CONVERTIR ALMAS, Y ENTIEÑDEAN LA BIBLIA Y LAS ENSENANZAS DE LA IGLESIA MUY BIEN. ENTONCES POR EJEMPLO EL NUMERO 7 EN UNA MAPA O EN SEQUIDA DE UN SENDERO DICE: AQUI ESTA UN CAMPAMENTO PARA REPOSO DE NOCHE, TOMADO DE LA BIBLIA DICE EN "EL DIA 7 DESCANSO". TAMBIEN EL SIMBOLO PARA EL NUMERO 1 ERA UN PUNTO O UN CIRCULO CERRADO. EL SIMBOLO PARA EL NUMERO UNO (1) TAMBIEN ES EL SIMBOLO PARA AGUA/FUENTES, Y TAMBIEN ES DE LA BIBLIA. "EN EL PRIMER DIA DIOS CREADO AQUA". ESTA INTRUDUCCION ESTABA TOMADA DEL LIBRO. "SEÑELES DE TESOROS, SIMBOLOS, Y SEÑALES DE SOMBRA Y SOL". POR ESTE AUTOR.

SI MAS EXACTO INFORMACION DE ARCHIVOS FUERA MAS DISPONIBLE PARA LOS CAZADORES DE TESOROS POR LOS, "ESCRITORES DE CUENTOS DE TESOROS: EN CUANTO DE MEDIDA/DISTANCIA, SEÑALES Y SIMBOLOS EN MAPAS Y EN EL COMPO, POSIBLE CIEN O MAS TESOROS Y MINAS SE HUBIERAN DISCUBRIDO EN MEJICO Y ARIZONA QUE ES UNO DE LOS MAS "RICOS" ESTADOS EN LOS ESTADOS UNIDOS.

A HORSE/ANIMAL CORRAL, **IF IT WAS CLOSE TO THE RANCH HOUSE,** WAS ONE OF THE VERY BEST HIDING PLACES BECAUSE THE ANIMALS' WEIGHT AND MOVEMENT WOULD QUICKLY PACK THE DIRT DOWN AFTER TREASURE WAS DEPOSITED OR RE-MOVED. ALSO YOU SHOULD CHECK OUT OLD "PIG STY" LOCATIONS.

UN CORRAL PAR UN CABALLO/ANIMAL, ESTABA CERCA DEL RANCHO, ERA UNO DE LOS MEJORES LUGARES, PORQUE LOS ANIMALS DESPUES DE DEPOSITO DEL TESORO ESTAMPAUAN LA TIERRA, TAMBIEN LUGARES DE PUERCOS

CORRAL

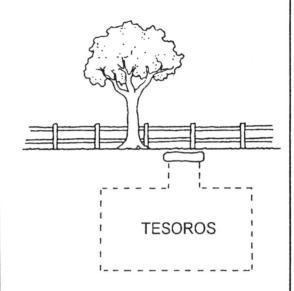

TESOROS

UNDER LARGE RANCH BARBEQUES WHERE THEY ROASTED SMALL CATTLE AND OTHER ANIMALS FOR "FIESTAS" AND SPECIAL OCCASIONS IS ANOTHER GREAT LOCATION USED BY MANY AS THEIR PRIVATE BANK. THIS ONE WAS A FAVORITE OF PANCHO VILLA.

DEBAJO DE UNA BARBACOA GRANDE DONDE ASAVAN GANADO PEQUENOS Y OTROS ANIMALS PARA "FIESTAS" Y OCASIONES ESPECIALES ES OTRA BUENA LOCALIDAD USADO POR MUCHOS, COMO BANCO PRIVADA ESTE ERA UN FAVORITO DE PANCHO VILLA

BARBACOA

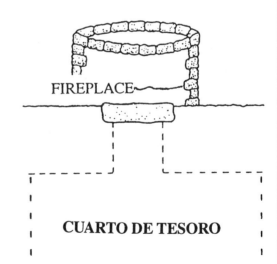

FIREPLACE

CUARTO DE TESORO

MANY ROCK WALLED WATER WELLS HAVE TREASURE ROOMS **IN USE TODAY** IN ISOLATED AREAS AROUND THE WORLD, ESPECIALLY **MEXICO**. THE ROCK COVERED ENTRANCE WILL USUALLY BE MID POINT BETWEEN THE GROUND LEVEL AND THE WATER LEVEL.

MUCHAS FUENTES DE AGUA CON PAREDES DE PIEDRA TANAN CUARTOS DE TESORO EN USO TODAVIA EN LUGARS ISLADO ALREDEDOR DEL MUNDO ESPECIALMENTE MEJICO. LA PUERTA ESTA LOCALIZADA EN EL MEDIO PUNTO DE AGUA Y LA TIERA.

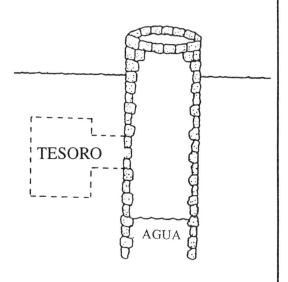

POZO DE AGUA

TESORO

AGUA

UNDER AN OLD FIREPLACE WAS SURELY THE MOST COMMON HIDING PLACE FOR VALUABLES AND TREASURES. USUALLY A FIRE WAS ALWAYS LIT TO HEAT COFFEE, COOK AND HEAT THE ROOM, AND SELDOM WAS THIS LOCATION CHECKED BY THIEVES AND ROBBERS.

DEBAJO DE UN HORNO DE PIEDRA ERA UNO DE LOS MAS COMUN LUGARES PARA ESCONDER OBJETOS VALIOSOS Y TESOROS. LA LUMBRE ESTABA PARA EL CAFE, COMIDA Y CALENTADOR PARA EL CUARTO, Y LADRONES CASI NUNCA BUSCABAN EN LOS HORNOS.

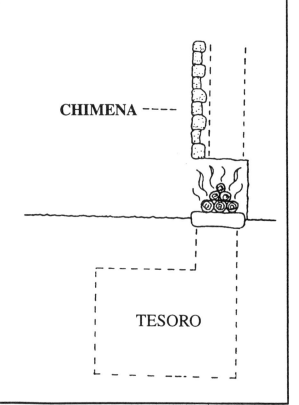

CHIMENA - - - -

TESORO

ORO: CUANDO HANDEN EN EL COMPO QUE TIENE ARBOLES DE PINO LOS CONOS ESTAN COLGANDO, BUSCAN POR ARBOLES SIN CONOS O CONOS NOMAS EN EL TRONCO. ARSENICO O MERCURIO ESTAN ALREDEDOR EN DIFERENTE GRADOS, TODOS LOS MINERALES CON ORO PARECE QUE AFECTAN (VAPORES) DIRECTO CONOS DE PINO.

PLATA: QUEDANCE CONSTANTEMENTE EN ALERTA POR "MALAS HIERBAS DE SULFURO". EXISTEN DONDE SULFURO FILTRA PARA ARRIBA DE LA TIERRA. ALGUNAS VECES SE HALLAN LINEA DE MALA HIERBA DE SULFURO CRECE PARA ABAJO DE UNA LOMA SIQUINDO UNA FAULTA O VENA. NOTA: HAY OTROS SULFUROS APARTE DE "SULFUROS DE PLATA", PERO SE HARIAN DE VER.

FAULTAS Y VENAS: NO TODO EL TIEMPO SE INDICAN EN TOPOGRAFIA COMO ARROYO O LINEAS DE DEPRESION. FAULTAS DETEÑEN HUMEDAD/AQUA ALREDEDOR. ADAMAS ARBOLES, SAGUAROS Y HASTA ARBUSTOS, ARRIBA O EN SEQUIDA, VAN A SER MAS GRANDE TAMAÑO COMO ARBOLES SERCA DE UN ARROYO CON AQUA SON MAS GRANDE. BUSCAN UN SENDERO O GRUPO MAS "GORDO" O MAS GRANDE.

AREA DE MINAS ESPAÑOLA: BUSCAN UNA AREA ESTERIL (EN RELACION A LA AREA ALREDEDOR) QUE ESTA "LISA" PUDEA SER UN "PATIO" DONDE LOS MINEROS USABAN "MERCURIO" (COMIENZANDO EN LOS 1560's) PARA RECUBRIR ORO DE MINERALES DE BAJO GRADO. EL MERCURIO COMPLETAMENTE MATA EL CRECER DE PLANTAS ALREDEDOR DE LAS AREA. NOTA: ALGUNAS VECES EN LECHO DE ROCA O EN DEPOSITOR DE BORAX TAMBIEN CAUSA AREAS ESTERIL.

CONSEJO ESPAÑOL: EN LOS 1560's Y LOS 70's ESPAÑA HISO MUCHOS DIBIJOS Y ESCULTURA EN MADERA REPRESENTANDO "COMO HACER" Y DESARROLLAR MINAS, APUNTALAR, VENTI-LACION, ETC. TAMBIEN HICIERON UNA LISTA DE CONSEJOS PARA LOS PROSPECTORES/EXPLORADORES EN QUE PONER ATENCION BUSCANDO. AQUI ESTAN UNOS POCOS: 1. BUSCAN DONDE LAS

LOMAS/MONTANAS, ESTAN MAS ESCABROSAS EN LINEA CON EL CIELO.

2. DEN ESPECIAL ATENCION HASTA MEDIA LIGA (UNA MIA) DE TODOS LOS "FUENTES" (FALTA). 3. BUSCAN AREAS CON EXCESIVO TAMAÑO EN LAS ALTAS MONTAÑAS. 4. BUSCAN TIERRAS CON COLOR "NARANJO" O PALIDO VERDE O QUEMADO COLOR.

ZAHORI: DE LOS 1500's HASTA EL MEDIO DE LOS 1600's LOS ESPAÑOLES USABAN VARILLAS DE ZAHORI PARA HALLAR MINERALES DE ORO Y PLATA. ELLOS PENSAVAN QUE "ZAHORI" ERA EL MEJOR MODO DE PROSPECTAR POR MUCHOS AÑOS. LOS ESPAÑOLES PARECE QUE TIENEN MUCHO EXITO EN HALLAR MINERALES EN ESTA MANERA COMO POR CIEN ANOS, ENTONCES DE REPENTE CAMBIARON A MAS BASICO MODOS DE PROSPECTAR. NO SAMBAMOS PORQUE DEJARON EL USO DE ZAHORI, UNOS ESPAÑOLES LO USABAN BIEN - POSIBLE QUE TRABAJE PARA USTED.

PIEDRA DE TESORO REFUGIO: (EN LA PAGINE XX) ESTOS GRANDE PEÑASCOS "PARA-DOS" FUERON CONSTRUIDOS POR PIRATAS Y OFRECEN LA CARA AL MAR. PARA AVISO QUE AVIA PROTECION Y AN-CLADERO EN EL PUNTO DEL LA COSTA. EL RENOVAR/HUE-COS AREA CORTADA EN EL PEÑASCO ERA PERFECTO RE-FUGIO DE LAS LLUVIAS PARA 4-6 PERSONAS. LOS ESPAÑOLES USABAN ESTOS MONUMENTOS PARA CUBIER PUERTAS DE MINAS, PERO MAS DEL TIEMPO ERA PARA ESCONDER TESOROS O MIN-

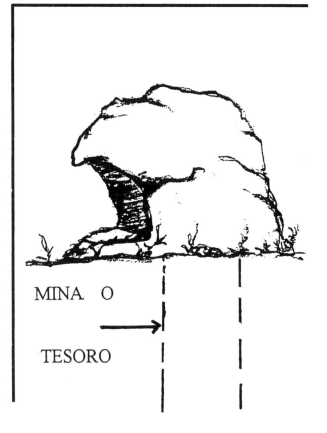

MINA O

TESORO

ERALES RICOS. PUESTOS EN AQUJEROS HONDOS ABAJO DEL CENTRO DEL PEÑASCO. TAMBIEN ESTE MONUMENTO ESTABA USADO EN LLANOS COMO UN "MONUMENTO ALPHA", PERO SUPESTO ABAJO DESTE PEÑASCO NO MAS ESTABA UN MENSAJE QUE DECIA BUSCAN EN EL "OMEGA PENASCO", ALLI ES EL ESCONDIDA/REFUGIO DE LA MINA O TESORO.

LA MAYORIA DE LOS SIMBOLOS EN MAPAS DE TESORO/MINAS SON DERIVADOS DE LA BIBLA. EN TEIMPOS ANTES, LOS JUDIOS USABAN SEÑALES, SIMBOLOS Y REFERENCIAS DEL ANTIGUO TESTAMENTO PARA ESCONDER QUE SIGNIFICA DE GENTE QUE VA OPRIMIR. LA IGLESIA PRIMERO HISO LO MISMO Y DESARROLO MAS POR MUCHOS AÑOS. NUMERISTAS "RELIGIOSIS" ERAN LOS MEJORES HACEDORES DE MAPAS Y EN TIEMPO DIBUJAVAN MAPAS BISICAS DE TESOROS O MINAS ESCONDIDAS ANTES DE QUE LAS MINAS SE HAGAN DESCUBRIDO O TESOROS ESCONDIDOS, DESPUES HACEN LAS MINAS/TESOROS ADAPTAR PARA EL CODIS EN LA MAPA.

MAPAS NUMEROSAS TIENEN DIBUJOS DE MATEO, MARCOS, LUCAS Y JUAN SIMBOLOS DE "IGLESIA" UNOS MAS COMUN SON:

UN "HOMBRE CON ALAS" REPRESENTA "MATEO"

UN "LEON CON ALAS" REPRESENTA "MARCOS"

UN "BUEY O CALVES CON ALAS" REPRESENTA "LUCAS"

LA AQUILA REPRESENTA "JUAN", TAMBIEN EL NUMERO "4" ES EL SIMBOLO DE JUAN.

SI CUALQUIERA DESTAS FIGURAS ESTAN EN UNA MAPA LE DICE UNA DE DOS COSAS O LAS DOS COSAS:

A. SI EL SIMBOLO ES CERCA DE DOS A CUATRO NUMEROS, QUIERE DECIR MIRAN PARA LA BIBLA. USANDO EL DOS A CUATRO NUMEROS PARA HALLAR EL CAPITULO Y VERSO DEL EVAGELIO ESCRITO POR ESA FIGURA, QUE LE DICE LAS DISTANCIA, DIRECCION O LO QUE QUIERE SABER.

B. MUCHOS TIEMPOS SI UNOS DESTOS SIMBOLOS ESTAN EN LA CABEZA, FONDO O PARA EL LADO DE LA MAPA, DICE QUE LA FIGURA ES EL PATRONO DEL HACEDOR DE MAPAS ORDEN DE RELIGION.

C. EL SIMBOLO MAS COMUN USADO EN MAPAS AQUI EN LOS ESTADOS UNIDOS Y EN MEJICO ERA LA "AQUILA", "JUAN".

TAMBIEN ERA EL UNICO SIMBOLO QUE SE PUEDE HALLAR EN EL SITIO DEL LA MINA/TESORO PORQUE DICE UN CUENTO DENTRO EL MISMO Y DA DIRECCIONS: SI USTAD ENCONTRA UNA AQUILA TRINCHADA, POR EJEMPLO EN UNA PIEDRA GRANDE, ENFRENTE DE LA AQUILA, DE UNA MIRADA A LA IZQUIERDA DEL PUNTO DE LA ALA IZQUIERDA, ENTONCES DE UNA MIRADA PARA ARRIBA, FORMANDO UNA LINEA MENTAL PARA ARRIBA DEL LA LOMA O DONDE QUIERA ESA DIRECCION SE LLEVA, PORQUE ALLI ES DONDE ESTA EL TESORO, O QUIZAS EN ESA LINEA HALLARAS UN MARCADOR FINAL. EL SIGNIFICADO RELIGASO SUCEDE DE LA CRUCIFICACION, "JUAN" ES MOSTRADO EN EL PIE DE LA CRUZ. PARA LA IZQUIERDA DE "JUAN" ESTA LA CRUZ Y ALTO EN LA CRUZ ESTA JESUS, ALTO PARA LA IZQUIERDA DE JUAN. ENTONCES: AQUI EN LA IZQUIERDA DE JUAN Y MAS ARRIBA ESTA EL "TESORO" (JESUS). EL SIGNIFICATIVO DOBLE Y EL MENSAJE DE LA AQUILA ES MUY CLARO PARA EL CREYENTE Y NO ES SIGNIFICANTE PARA EL QUE NO CREA QUE ESTABA QUERINDO A INTERPRETAR UNA MAPA EN CODIO.

DENTGA EN SU MENTE DE QUE EN GENERAL, LA IGLESIA, LOS "RELIGOSOS" Y LOS ESCOLASTICO BIBLICOS QUE AYUDARON EN DESIGNIO/CODIO DE MAPAS, PORQUE ESTABAN BIEN VERSADOS EN SIMBOLISMO, ETC., Y ESTABAN SOLICITADOS PARA AYUDAR POR DUEÑOS DE MINAS Y ESPAÑA. NO QUIERE DECIR O REFLECTAR EN CUALQUIER MODO QUE ELLOS O LA "IGLESIA" ERAN DUEÑOS EN LA MAPAS, MINAS O TESOROS — PERO QUIEN SABE?

UNA COSA POR CIERTO EN CUANTO DE LA IGLESIA, MISIONES Y MINERA. AMBOS ESPAÑOLES Y MINEROS MEJICANOS Y LOS DUEÑOS DE LAS MINAS ERAN MUY GENEROSOS CON LA IGLESIA, Y PAGABAN POR MUCHOS EDIFICIOS Y MUEBLES DE MUCHAS MISIONES. EN UNAS OCASIONES LOS DUEÑOS DE LAS MINAS DABAN UN PERCENTAJE ESPECIFICO DEL INGRESO DE LAS MINAS PARA LA MISIONS LOCAL.

EN AÑOS PASADOS AMOS HALLADO CINCO SANTUARIOS. QUATRO DE LOS CINCO ERAN LO MISMO QUE ESTE DIBUJO. EL NUMERO CINCO ERA UNA CUEVA CONVERTIDA. EN EL SANTUARIO EN LA CUEVA POR ACCIDENTE HALLAMOS LOS TRINCHAR/ESCULTURA PIEDRAS DOSEL. ERAN COMO UNA PULGADA Y MEDIA DE ESPESO Y COMO 9 PULGADAS A 14 PULGADAS DE ANCHO. ERAN COLORADAS (HEMITITO), POSIBLE USADA PRO SU BELLEZA, Y PESABA COMO 23 LIBRAS CADA UNA.

SANTUARIOS DE MINAS

CADA MINA TIENEA UN SANTUARIO CERCAS DEL LA ENTRADA. LO MISMO UNA PEQUEÑA OPERACION DE DOS A CINCO HOMBRES TIENEA UN "LUGAR" CERCAS PARA LA DIARIA ORACION. EL SANTUARIO CONTENIA UNA CRUZ SENCILLA. O POR UNA MINA GRANDE PODIN CONTENIAR UNA CRUZ Y EN ESTATUA. EL TRABAJO DEL MINERO ERA PELIGROSO Y UNA ORACION EN FRENTE DEL SANTUARIO ANTES DE ENTRAR A LA MINA Y OTRA VEZ DESPUES DE SALIR UN ORACION DE GRACIAS ERA UNA COSA DARIA.

SUBYUGADO AL TERRENO, EL SANTUARIO VARIAVA. PODIA SER ESPACIO ANGOSTO ENTRE DOS PIEDRAS O UNA CUEVA CONVERTIDA PARA LOS "FRAY/FRAILES" "CASA DEL DIA, QUE LOS MINEROS PREFERIAN PORQUE EL PADRE ESTA CERCAS PARA AUDAR A LOS LASTIMADOS, Y PARA OIR LAS ULTIMAS PALABRAS ANTES DE MORIR. LAS LEYES DE ESPAÑA REQUERIMIENTO QUE EL SANTUARIO ESTABA SITUADO ENTRE 200 VARAS (SOLDADOS/EN PIE) DEL LA ENTRADA A LA MINA.

UN SANTUARIO ERAN COMO 3 A 5 PIES DE ANCHO, Y COMO 2 A 2-1/2 PIES DE ONDO Y 4 A 6 PIES DE ALTO. LA CUMBRE DEL SANTUARIO TODO EL TIEMPO ESTABA CURVADA. FREQUENTE PONEIAN UN DOSEL EN LA RADIA DE LA CURVA Y SALIA DE LA PARED COMO IO PULGADAS, HECHA DE MADERA O PIEDRA. SI HALLAN AGUJEROS TALADOROS ENTRE LA TOPA DE LA (CURVA) DE UN POSIBLE SANTUARIO, ENTONCES SABEN POR SIERTO.

LOS MINEROS QUITABAN EL DOSEL Y LA CRUZ/ESTATUA Y LAS ESCONDIAN CUANDO SE PARTIAN POR UN TIEMPO EL LUGAR DE RODILLAS ESTABA HASTA CUARENTA PIES DE CUADRADO.

PEQUEÑOS DOS A CINCO HOMBRES ESPAÑOLES Y MEJICANO TUNELES MINAS FREQUENTE TENIAN UN "CUARTO" GRANDE COMO 15 PIES DENTRO EL TUNEL Y SERVIA PARA MUCHOS MODOS COMO PARA ALMACENAR EQUIPO, JARROS DE AGUA Y COMIDA, ETC., Y TAMBIEN UN ESTANTE O CORTE EN UNA PARED AL LADO QUE CONTENIA UN ESTATUA O UN CRUSIFIJO Y UNA CANDELA QUE SERVIA COMO UN SANTUARIO PARA ELLOS.

EL LUGAR ESCONDIDO PARA MINERALES DE ORO Y PLATA Y LINGOTES EN UNA MINA DE TUNELES PEQUEÑOS ESTABA SITUADA EN EL SUELO DEL CUARTO DIRECTO DEBAJO DEL REPISA O MUESCA (SANTUARIO) CON ESPERANZA QUE EL SANTUARIO FUERA EL PROTECTORATE DE LAS PROPIEDADES DE ELLOS. EL OTRO LUGAR IMPORTANTE PARA BUSCAR TESOROS EN TUNELES Y CUEVAS ES INMEDIATEMENTE EN LA ENTRADA AL TUNEL O CUEVA. MUCHAS VECES EN LA ENTRADA DE UNA

CUEVA DONDE LOS MINEROS VIVIAN SE ENCONTRARAN UNA
LINEA DE PIEDRAS. ESTAS PIEDRAS ESTABAN CALENTADAS EN LA
TARDE Y PUESTAS EN LA PUERTA DE LA CUEVA PARA GUARDAR
QUE CULEBRAS Y OTRO ANIMALES NO ENTRARAN. ES ABAJO DE
ESTAS PIEDRAS DONDE ESTABA UNA "MUESCA" DE AGUJERO
ESTABA HECHO PARA ESCONDAR LOS TESOROS DE ELLOS.

EL SEÑAL, SIMBOLO O NUMERO MAS GRANDE O PALABRA, FIGURA EN UNA MAPA COMO DE COSTUMBRE ES LA "LLAVE" O "INDICIO" DEL CODIO DE LA MAPA O DEL CREADOR DE MAPAS. ESTE ALERTO PARA CUALQUIERA LETRA EN UNA PALABRA QUE ES MAS GRANDE O MAS PEQUEÑA. QUE OTRAS LETRAS EN LA PALABRA. DE GRAN IMPORTANCIA REVISE CADA LETRA "A" PARA VER SI LA BARRA CRUZADA ESTA EN UN ANGULO. LA LETRA "A" ES UNA PALABRA EN ESPAÑOLE QUE QUIRE DECIR "VAYA-PARA-EN". MIRE "LETRAS/DOCUMENTOS EN CODIO PARA TESOROS".

LOS "CODIOS" DE MEJICO ERAN MAS O MENOS LO MISMO COMO LAS DE ESPAÑA CON UNOS COMBIOS MENORES. ESTOS ESTABAN COMPILADOS EN 1826 Y DURANTE LOS 26 ANOS DEL REINADO DE MEJICO SOBRE EL TERRENO QUE AHORA ES LOS ESTADOS UNIDOS. MEJICO NO PODIA HACER CUMPLIR REGLAS DE MINERA. MAS DE LAS FAMILAS MEJICANAS QUE ERAN MINEROS O HACIENDAS USABAN LOS CODIS "VIEJOS" AUMENTABAN O CAMBIBAN UN POCO PARA "NO MAS FAMILA" ENTENDIMIENTO.

DETENGA EN SU MENTE QUE LOS ESPAÑOLES (EN ESPAÑA) FUERON CONQUISTADOS POR ROMA Y DOMINADO POR LOS "MORO'S". POR LA INFLUENCIA DE LOS DOS, ROMANO'S Y LOS ARABES COMO ESCRITURAS, PALABRAS Y NUMEROS ESTABAN BIEN CONOCIDOS Y MUY USADOS O INTERCAMBIDOS POR LOS ESPAÑOLES EN LAS MAPAS, LETRAS Y DOCUMENTOS.

NUNCA VA HALLER MARCAS, SEÑALES O INDICADORES DIRECTAMENTE SOBRE LA ENTRADA A LA MINA O TESORO. ESTA ERA UNA REGLA CARDENAL DE LOS ESPAÑOLES Y CONTINUODO POR LOS MEJICANOS. NUNCA PERMITIAN MARCAS IINSIGNIFI-CANTE O PEQUEÑAS EN EL PUNTO EXACTO EN EL LUGAR ESCONDIDO. DE RESULTO DE ESTA LEY "TRAINGULOS" ERAN LOS FAVORITO MARCAS DE LOS ESPAÑOLES Y ESTABAN CONSTRUIDOS CERCAS DE LA LOCALIDAD DE LA MINA/TESORO, USADO COMO EL "BASE" POR EXACTO MEDIADAS PARA ESTE MINA/TESORO.

SI USTED SE CIENTE QUE "SABE" QUE AREA LA MAPA DESCRIBE O REPRESENTA, PERO LA TOPOGRAFIA NO CONFORME, PONGA LA MAPA AL REVES, EL NORTE PUEDE SER

"SUR", ALGUNAS VECES UN "RIO" TAL VEZ NO SEA UN RIO SINO UN RIACHUELO DE TEMPORADA O UN "DESAGUE" O COLOCA EL MAPA FRENTE A UN ESPEJO PARA QUE LO VEAS AL REVES. LAS IMAGENES DE MAPAS DE AGUA/ESPEJO FUERON MUY COMUNES. SI NO TODO EL MAPA, ENTONCES SOLO UNA **PORCION** DEL MAPA PUEDE SER UNA **IMAGEN DE ESPEJO.**

SIMBOLOS, SEÑALES Y NUMEROS FUERON USADOS **MAS DE UNA VEZ (REUSADOS)** CUANTO FUE POSIBLE EN UN MAPA, PARA PODER DAR MAS DE UN SIGNIFICADO O MENSAJE.

EL ALFA Y EL OMEGA (EL **MAS IMPORTANTE** MONUMENTO EN LA PRADERA). **CUALQUIER** MINA, TESORO/ESCONDIDO ESPAÑOL, **SE PUEDE ENCONTRAR SIN UN DETECTOR DE METALES O EQUIPO ELECTRONICO, SI ES QUE USTED ENCUENTRA PRIMERO EL "ALFA",** PORQUE **EL OMEGA ESTA EN EL TESORO DE LA MINA.** POR CONSIGUIENTE COMPLETANDO Y REFLEXIONANDO EN LA CITA BILBICA " YO SOY EL ALFA Y EL OMEGA", "YO SOY EL PRINCIPIO Y EL FIN", "YO SOY EL PRIMERO Y EL ULTIMO". LOS ESPAÑOLES ADEMAS DE CONSTRUIR Y PONER MONUMENTOS PARA Y DE LA MINA Y/O TESORO, FUERON REQUERIDOS POR ESPAÑA **A QUE INSTALARAN ALFAS Y OMEGAS.**

SI EL "ALFA" (MONUMENTO DE ENTRADA AL SENDERO) TIENE LA FORMA DE UN **CORAZON**, HABRA OTRO "CORAZON" ("EL OMEGA") EN LA MINA/TESORO. **CUALQUIERA LA FIGURA /FORMA DEL MONUMENTO ALFA,** SERA REPETIDA (LA MISMA) AL **FINAL DEL SENDERO.** EL MONUMENTO "ALFA" PUEDE SER DE CUALQUIER DISEÑO - PUEDE SER UNA CABEZA INDIA, UNA ROCA CUBRIENDO EL TESORO, UNA X GRANDE, UNA CABEZA DE CABALLO, ETC, ETC. -LO QUE FUERA MAS FACIL DE CONSTRUIR E IGUALAR CON LA GEOLOGIA AL PRINCIPIO Y AL FINAL DEL SENDERO.

UN ARCHIVISTA (DE ROMA) ME CONTO LA SIGUIENTE HISTORIA.
PARECE SER QUE UN CIERTO "REY" DE ESPAÑA A MEDIADOS DE LOS
1500 TENIA UNA GRAN OPINION DE SU ESTADO Y TAMAÑO FISICO. EL
REY ESTABA INVOLUCRADO EN PONER Y AJUSTAR "EL SISTEMA DE
MEDIDAS DE ESPAÑA" **PARA MINAS Y TESOROS SOLAMENTE,** ASI
ES QUE, NATURALMENTE, LLAMO A SU SASTRE PARA QUE LE
AYUDARA EN ESTE GRAN PROBLEMA QUE TENIA ENTRE MANOS.
CINCO DE LAS SEIS MEDIDAS "REALES" ERAN: 1. BRAZA 5'7", LA
DISTANCIA ENTRE LA PUNTA DE LOS DEDOS CON EL BRAZO DEL REY
ESTIRADO. 2. ESTADO 5'7", LA ALTURA DE UN HOMBRE (LA SUYA).
3. VARA 33", LA LINEA DE SU CINTURA Y DISTANCIA DE PASO (DE
PUNTA A TALON). 4. CODO (1/2 VARA) 16 1/2", DE LA PUNTA DE SU
CODO A LA PUNTA DE SU DEDO MEÑIQUE (ESTIRADOS). 5. PALMO 8
1/4", LA DISTANCIA ENTRE LA PUNTA DE SU MEÑIQUE Y EL DEDO
PULGAR DE LA MANO, CON LA PALMA ABIERTA Y ESTIRADA. ESTE
ARCHIVISTA NUNCA HA VISTO ESTE DOCUMENTO, PERO FUE
INFORMADO POR OTRO ARCHIVISTA DE SU EXISTENCIA. UNA
HISTORIA MUY INTERESANTE, ME DIJE, Y AUN MAS POR ESTAS
MEDIDAS ESPECIALIZADAS "REALES" SON LAS MEDIDAS
ESCLUSIVAS USADAS EN LOS MAPAS DE TESOROS DE ESPAÑA. LA
LEY DE ESPAÑA REQUIERE QUE ESTAS MEDIDAS SEAN USADAS EN
TODOS SUS MAPAS DE TESOROS/MINAS PARA EL NUEVO MUNDO Y
QUE **NUNCA** FUERAN CAMBIADAS. (PERU, COLOMBIA, PANAMA,
GUATEMALA, MEXICO, ETC.)

ES VERDAD QUE ESPAÑA CAMBIO SU SISTEMA DE MEDIDAS Y
DISTANCIAS DURANTE SUS 350 AÑOS DE GOBIERNO EN EL NUEVO
MUNDO; SIN EMBARGO, LOS CAMBIOS **NO AFECTARON A LOS
MAPAS DE TESOROS Y MINAS NI LAS MEDIDAS DE LOS MAPAS.**
LAS SIGUIENTES MEDIDAS PERMANECIERON **CONSTANTES.**

LEGUA	LA LEGUA NAUTICA TENIA 3.27 MILLAS Y LA VARIABLE, DEBIDO A LA CORRIENTE (BOTE A LA DERIVA) ERA CONSIDERADA COMO DE 3.18 A 3.27. LA DE ESTATUTO (TIERRA) ERA DE 2.18 MILLAS; LA VARIABLE ERA CONSIDERADA COMO DE 2.1 A 2.18. DOS LEGUAS NAUTICAS ERAN IGUALES APROXIMADAMENTE A TRES LEGUAS DE ESTATUTO. NAUTICA = OCEANO, DE ESTATUTO = TIERRA
BRAZA	LA BRAZA ERA DE 5 PIES 7 PULGADAS, USADA BASICAMENTE PARA AGUAS PROFUNDAS. HOY EN DIA OTRO TIPO DE BRAZA SE USA, QUE TIENE 6 PIES. MARINEROS Y PIRATAS USABAN LAS "BRAZAS" COMO MEDIDAS DE DISTANCIA CUANDO SE ENTERRABAN TESOROS EN ISLAS A LO LARGO DE LAS LINEAS COSTERAS. SUS MAPAS DE TESOROS CASI NUNCA SE REFERIAN A PASOS O VARAS, A PESAR DE QUE EL MAPA DIJERA **"LUGARES"**.
UN ESTADO	COMO "UN ESTADO" SE CONOCIA A LA ALTURA DE UN HOMBRE, 5 PIES 7 PULGADAS, Y SE REFERIA A PROFUNDIDAD DE TIERRA. MINAS CUBIERTAS Y ESCONDIDAS ASI COMO GRANDES TESOROS, SE DEBIAN CUBRIR CON "UN ESTADO" O CON MULTIPLOS DE "UN ESTADO". UNA "BRAZA" ERA EL EQUIVALENTE NAUTICO EN DISTANCIA.
VARA	ESTA ES LA DIFICIL. HABIA MUCHAS DISTANCIAS CON "VARAS", YA QUE CADA ESTADO Y PROVINCIA DE ESPAÑA TENIA SUS PROPIAS MEDIDAS DE VARAS. DE MODO QUE ALGUNOS MAPAS USADOS POR LOS ESPAÑOLES TENIAN SUS EQUIVALENTES DE MEDIDAS NATIVOS, DE 30" A 35.9". AQUI, LOS MAPAS DE TESOROS/MINAS DEBIAN SER: LA VARA DE CAMINO (DE SOLDADO) ERA DE 33" **APROXIMADAMENTE**. LA VARA MEDIDA ES DE 33" **EXACTAMENTE**.

CODO	EL "CODO" ERA LA MITAD DE LA VARA - 16 1/2". ESTE SE REFERIA BASICAMENTE A AGUAS PROFUNDAS EN REPORTES/DOCUMENTOS DE TESOROS, Y A VECES EN MAPAS DONDE UN GALEON O TESORO ESTABAN HUNDIDOS. **NOTA:** TODAS LAS PROFUNDIDADES DE AGUA REPORTADAS ERAN SIEMPRE MEDIDAS EN **MAREA ALTA**.
PALMO	EL "PALMO" ERA LA MITAD DEL "CODO" - 8 1/4". APARECIA EN MAPAS DE TESOROS USUALMENTE PARA DESCRIBIR EL TAMAÑO DE LAS BARRAS DE ORO O PLATA. TAMBIEN, FRECUENTEMENTE EL "PALMO" ERA USADO AL HABLAR DE LA PROFUNDIDAD DE UN ARROYO O RIO QUE CONTENIA ORO.
VARA DE MEXICO	LA VARA MEXICANA FUE FIRMEMENTE ESTABLECIDA EL 4 DE ENERO DE 1823, TRAS EL REINADO ESPAÑOL, EN 32.8 PULGADAS. SIN EMBARGO, POR LAS CONSTANTES REVUELTAS EN MEXICO Y LA DESORGANIZACION DE MUCHOS MINEROS/MINAS, LAS ANTIGUAS SEÑALES, SIMBOLOS Y MEDIDAS ESTABAN AUN EN USO. EN ESE TIEMPO MUCHAS NUEVAS SEÑALES O SIGNIFICADOS DE SEÑALES FUERON AÑADIDAS DE FORMA PRIVADA A LA "FAMILIA" DE LOS MAPAS GUARDADOS.
LUGARES - DISTANCIAS	CUANDO ALGUNA DE ESTAS PALABRAS, "LUGARES" Y/O "DISTANCIAS", ESTAN USADAS EN UN MAPA O DOCUMENTO DE TESORO, NORMALMENTE SIGNIFICAN: A; LAS MEDIDAS **NO ESTAN** EN DISTANCIAS DE VARAS. B; SI UN "EXTRANJERO" HIZO EL MAPA, PODRIA SER UNA DISTANCIA COMUN CONOCIDA EN **SU** TIERRA NATAL, ALEMANIA, FRANCIA, ITALIA, ETC.

1. ORO, PLATA Y BARRAS DE ARENA

EL CAPITAN ISRAEL GRAY, UN FRANCES INDEPENDIENTE DE ESPAÑA Y DUEÑO DE UN BUEN BARCO, TRABAJO A LO LARGO DE LA COSTA OESTE Y EN EL GOLFO DE CALIFORNIA. TRANSPORTO MINEROS Y EQUIPO DE MINERIA Y CASI TODO LO NECESARIO ENTRE 1846 Y 1862. EL CAPITAN GRAY CONOCIO A MUCHOS MINEROS Y SE LE CONOCIA COMO COMPRADOR, SI EL PRECIO ERA BUENO, DE ORO Y PLATA DE ALTA CALIDAD (ROBADO) O DE MINEROS. EL CAPITAN GRAY HABIA CONVERTIDO SU METAL EN BARRAS O LINGOTES DE 60 A 80 LIBRAS, LAS CUALES TENIA LA INTENCION DE LLEVARSE A ESPAÑA CUANDO DEJARA LAS AGUAS MEXICANAS. PERO EN 1862 SURGIERON MUCHOS PROBLEMAS Y TUVO QUE PARTIR DE MEXICO CON TANTA RAPIDEZ QUE NO LE DIO TIEMPO DE RECOBRAR SU TESORO ENTERRADO. UNOS AÑOS MAS TARDE EL CAPITAN GRAY MURIO EN ESPAÑA Y DENTRO DE SU BARCO FUE ENCONTRADA UNA CARTA QUE HABIA ESCRITO. AQUI ESTA LA INFORMACION DE LA LOCALIDAD DEL TESORO:

QUERIDO KINSMAN:

"... SI, NO SOLO ME TEMIA EL TIEMPO QUE REQUERIRIA SACAR MI TESORO Y LA TARDANZA QUE MI PARTIDA PODRIA CAUSAR, A MI ME HA DADO TEMOR REGRESAR POR EL Y NO CONFIO EN OTROS PARA QUE LO HAGAN POR MI. ES TODO TUYO - 16 BARRAS DE ORO Y 38 DE PLATA ENTERRADAS EN UNA PEQUEÑA ISLA DE 3 ACRES. MUY PARECIDA A LA BARRA DE ARENA EN EL RIO BALUARTE, NO MUY LEJOS DE LA COSTA DEL GOLFO DE CALIFORNIA, ENTRE EL GOLFO Y ROSARIO, SINALOA, MEXICO, (MAS O MENOS A 40 MILLAS AL SUR DE MAZATLAN). EL ENTIERRO ESTA CERCA DE LA PARTE BAJA DEL FINAL DE LA ISLA Y A MEDIO CAMINO ENTRE DOS ARBOLES DE BUEN TAMAÑO. CONSIDERA LA POSIBILIDAD, COMO YO HICE, DE OFRECER A LA IGLESIA LA MITAD DE LO QUE ENCUENTRES SI ELLOS TE PROTEGEN Y TE EMBARCAN DE REGRESO ALLI, CON ALGUNOS DE LOS PADRES, PARA LOGRAR LA RECUPERACION". NOTA: SI EL TESORO AUN ESTA ALLI, YO PENSARIA QUE UN VIAJE DE "PESCA" DE

3 O 4 DIAS HACIA EL RIO BALUARTE CON UN PAR DE DETECTORES DE METAL, PODRIA PAGAR EN GRANDE.

2. DEPOSITO DE ORO TAN GRANDE COMO UNA CASA

EN UN CAÑON BAJO "LA MESA ENCANTADA" ESCARPADO DE ALTAS PAREDES YACE UNA PILA GIGANTE DEL PRECIOSO METAL DE ORO DEL TAMAÑO DE UNA CASA. PROVISIONES PARA LA MINA Y LOS MINEROS FUERON TRAIDAS POR EL GOLFO DE CALIFORNIA A UN PUNTO COSTERO 93 MILLAS AL SUR DE LA CABEZA DEL GOLFO, DESDE DONDE LOS MINEROS CARGARIAN LAS PROVISIONES TIERRA ADENTRO HASTA LA MINA, DIA Y MEDIO DE VIAJE. ESTALLO UNA PEQUEÑA REVOLUCION, Y EL BARCO QUE LLEVABA LAS PROVISIONES A LOS MINEROS FUE UTILIZADO POR ALGUN OFICIAL PARA OTROS USOS. DESPUES DE SEIS MESES DE NO TENER PROVISIONES, LOS MINEROS DECIDIERON IRSE. TODOS ELLOS SE LLEVARON UN POCO DEL METAL DE ORO CON ELLOS Y DECIDIERON SEGUIR UN CAÑON QUE LOS LLEVO HASTA LA COSTA DEL GOLFO, Y DE AHI A LA MAS CERCANA COMUNIDAD "GUAYMAS". LOS OFICIALES EN GUAYMAS LOS ARRESTARON INMEDIATAMENTE, LES QUITARON EL ORO Y LOS EMBARCARON DE REGRESO. SU HISTORIA FUE BIEN DOCUMENTADA, PERO LA MINA Y EL GRAN PILAR DE ORO ("LA CASA") AUN NO SE ENCUENTRAN. LA MINA ESTA EN UN LARGO CAÑON QUE SE LLEGA CERCA DE LA PARTE ESTE DE LA MESA. ES UN TERRENO ESCABROSO, Y UN AEROPLANO PEQUEÑO O LUZ INFRARROJA PODRIA ENCONTRAR EL PUNTO.

3. TESORO PIRATA

EL TESORO PIRATA FUE ENTERRADO CERCA DEL BANCO NORTE DEL RIO SONORA A MENOS DE 5 MILLAS ADENTRO DEL GOLFO DE CALIFORNIA. ES MUY POSIBLE QUE LOS INDIOS SERI LO CAMBIARAN DE LUGAR Y LO ESCONDIERAN EN TIBURON. SIN EMBARGO, SI AUN ESTA ALLI, SERIA MUY SENCILLO DE ENCONTRAR. UNA GRAN ROCA PLANA O UN ACANTILADO VIENDO HACIA EL LADO DEL RIO TIENE UN SIMBOLO DE ANCLA DE CUATRO BRAZAS (23') DE DIAMETRO INCRUSTADO. Y ESTA A MENOS DE 300 PIES DE LA PARTE NORTE DEL RIO. EL TIMONEL DEL BARCO PORTUGUES CONTO DE ESTE TESORO

AL PADRE QUE ESCUCHO SU ULTIMA CONFESION, ANTES DE SER COLGADO POR PIRATERIA DOS AÑOS DESPUES DE QUE EL TESORO FUE ENTERRADO.

4. TESORO DEL MAR DE CORTEZ

EL RIO YAQUI TAMBIEN ESCONDE UN TESORO EN BARRAS DE ORO Y PLATA QUE ESTA A DOS MILLAS ADENTRO DEL GOLFO DE CALIFORNIA, Y A 200 PASOS DE DONDE SE HACE ANGOSTO EL RIO YAQUI Y FRENTE A LA VIEJA MISION JESUITA (CABECERA) "RAHUN" AL ESTE DE VISTA "POTAM". ESTAS BARRAS VINIERON DE LAS MINAS **ALEJADAS** DEL RIO YAQUI, EN DONDE ESPERABAN TRANSPORTACION POR BARCO. LA REBELION DE LOS YAQUIS CAUSO QUE LOS OFICIALES TRANSFIRIERAN EL TESORO YA CLASIFICADO A UNA CUEVA, Y DESPUES VOLARON LA ENTRADA PARA CERRARLA. FUE REPORTADO QUE LA PRINCIPAL RAZON POR LA QUE MOVIERON EL TESORO A LA CUEVA FUE PARA PROBAR A LOS OFICIALES DEL BARCO QUE NO LLEVABAN NADA DE CARGA, Y ASI ASEGURABAN SUFICIENTE ESPACIO EN EL BARCO PARA LLEVAR A TODOS LOS GUARDIAS, OFICIALES, MINEROS Y A SUS FAMILIAS QUE SE HABIAN JUNTADO EN LA COSTA DEL GOLFO AGUARDANDO RESCATE. NUNCA FUE ENCONTRADA LA CUEVA DE BARRAS. UN TERMINADOR-DOBLE PROFUNDO O UN RADAR QUE PENETRE LA TIERRA LO PODRIA LOCALIZAR HOY -- ¡ANIMATE!.

5. 100 MILLONES BAJO LA ALBERCA

EL GENERAL ANACLETO LOPEZ SOLIA DECIR: "TENGO SUFICIENTE TESORO PARA GENERAR UNA REVOLUCION EN MEXICO". EL GENERAL MURIO EN 1970. "Y CON MI AMIGO EL GENERAL BAÑUELOS DE VALVERDE PODRIAMOS PAGAR DOS REVOLUCIONES". PARECE SER QUE ESTOS DOS GENERALES ERAN MUY RICOS, PERO A PRINCIPIOS DE 1943 ANACLETO FUE A HABLAR CON UNO DE SUS VIEJOS AMIGOS, EL GENERAL MANUEL AVILA CAMACHO, QUIEN A SU VEZ ERA PRESIDENTE DE MEXICO. COMO GENERAL DE LA DIVISION, ANACLETO TENIA TODO EL PODER. LE PIDIO AL PRESIDENTE CAMACHO QUE LE PAGARA TODOS LOS GASTOS QUE HABIA TENIDO CON SUS TROPAS POR TANTOS AÑOS.

DESPUES CAMACHO MANDO A LA CASA DE ANACLETO EN LAS VIBORAS **DOS CAMIONES DE LA ARMADA CON BARRAS DE ORO,** " LA HACIENDA LAS VIBORAS".

ANACLETO RETUVO EL TESORO EN SU HACIENDA DOS SEMANAS APROXIMADAMENTE, PERO DESPUES DECIDIO TRANSPORTARLO A SU **OTRA** HACIENDA, NO SIN ANTES ENSEÑARSELO A TODA SU FAMILIA, INCLUYENDO A **SU HIJO ANACLETO.** TIEMPO DESPUES, EL GENERAL DECIDIO CONSTRUIR UNA ALBERCA (SOBRE LA TIERRA) EN SU SEGUNDA HACIENDA, EN DONDE VIVE SU AMANTE. EL ORO DE CAMACHO Y UNA ENORME CAJA FUERTE DE 4'X5'X8' ESTAN ESCONDIDOS EN LA SEGUNDA HACIENDA. EL PROMETIO DECIRLE A SU HIJO ANACLETO "QUE LE ENSEÑARIA EN DONDE ESTABA ESCONDIDO EL TESORO", PERO MURIO MIENTRAS DORMIA, Y NADIE SABE DONDE ESTA ESCONDIDO EL TESORO. TAL VEZ **BAJO** LA ALBERCA. ¿Y QUE HAY ACERCA DEL TESORO DEL GENERAL BAÑUELOS EN LA VIEJA HACIENDA VALVERDE? **HAZ UN PACTO** CON LAS FAMILIAS DE AMBOS GENERALES. -- Y OTRAS FAMILIAS DE OFICIALES Y GENERALES POLITICOS QUE HAN FALLECIDO. LES ASEGURO QUE LA MAYORIA DE ELLOS TENIAN UN TESORO ESCONDIDO, PORQUE EN AQUELLOS DIAS NADIE CONFIABA EN LOS BANCOS.

6. PEPITAS DE ORO DEL TAMAÑO DE UNA PERA

EN LA SIERRA MADRE, ENTRE LOS ESTADOS DE SONORA Y CHIHUAHUA, HAY UN LAGO QUE SE ENCUENTRA AL OESTE DEL RIO YAQUI. JUNTO AL LAGO, NO MUY LEJOS, HAY UN HORNO MUY ANTIGUO CON UN TERRAPLEN ESCORIADO DE PLATA Y COBRE. CERCA DEL HORNO, SE ENCONTRARON DOS PEPITAS DE ORO DEL TAMAÑO DE UNA PERA, JUNTO CON VARIAS HERRAMIENTAS. LA MINA DEBE DE ESTAR MUY CERCA, AUNQUE AUN NO HA SIDO ENCONTRADA. EL FEDERAL ENRICO MARTINEZ DIJO EN SU REPORTE, "PARECE QUE TENIAN MUCHA PRISA Y NUNCA REGRESARON"

7. EL TESORO DE MOCTEZUMA

ALGUNOS ESCRITORES OPINAN QUE EL TESORO DE MOCTEZUMA ESTA ESCONDIDO EN LOS ESTADOS UNIDOS, Y ESPECIFICAN LUGARES COMO UTAH, NUEVO MEXICO, ARIZONA Y OTROS NO MENCIONADOS. NUESTRAS INVESTIGACIONES INDICAN QUE SE ENCUENTRA AL SUR DE MONTERREY, EN MEXICO. ALGUNOS HECHOS A CONSIDERAR:

1. ALGUNOS DE LOS AZTECAS QUE FUERON TORTURADOS, DIERON LA MISMA INFORMACION QUE LA CARAVANA QUE PARTIO POR 43 DIAS AL NORTE DE MEXICO, Y LUEGO CAMBIANDO RUTA HACIA AL OESTE, CERCA DE UN GRAN LAGO, EN DONDE SE ADENTRARON A UN CAÑON EN MEDIO DE UNA GRAN MONTAÑA QUE TENIA 7 PICOS ALTOS, POR 4 Y 1/2 DIAS MAS. CERCA DEL FINAL DEL CAÑON HABIA **SIETE** CUEVAS, LAS CUALES HABIAN SIDO CERRADAS Y ESCONDIDAS. LAS REABRIERON, LAS LLENARON CON EL TESORO Y LAS VOLVIERON A CERRAR. SU REGRESO LES TOMO LA MITAD DEL TIEMPO Y SE HABIAN IDO POR 6 MESES.

2. LOS ESPAÑOLES PODIAN VIAJAR MAS O MENOS 32 MILLAS DIARIAS SIN EXCESO DE PESO. ENTONCES, CALCULARON QUE LOS AZTECAS VIAJARON 15 MILLAS DIARIAS DE IDA Y 30 MILLAS DIARIAS DE REGRESO, Y QUE EL TESORO SE ENCONTRARIA A 275 LEGUAS (605 MILLAS) AL NORTE Y 29 LEGUAS (63 MILLAS) AL OESTE, DENTRO DEL RANGO DE LA MONTAÑA.

3. DEBEMOS DE TENER PRESENTE QUE UNA LEGUA DE SOLDADO O DE CAMINO ERA DE 2.18 MILLAS DECRETADAS (NO DE 3 O 3.5).

4. PLATICAMOS CON ALGUNOS EMPLEADOS Y CARTOGRAFOS DEL MUSEO DE ANTROPOLOGIA EN LA CIUDAD DE MEXICO. ELLOS NOS DIERON **SUS PUNTOS DE VISTA** CON RESPECTO A LOS POSIBLES CAMINOS QUE LOS AZTECAS PODRIAN HABER

TOMADO PARA ESCONDER ESTE **INCREIBLE TESORO.**
ESTA LOCALIDAD ESTA A 150 MILLAS S.S.E. (AL SUR, SURESTE)
DE **"MONTERREY"** EN LA PARTE MEDIA SUPERIOR DE LA
SECCION 132 DE O.N.C., MAPA J-24 Y DIRECTAMENTE AL
SURESTE DEL GRAN LAGO.

8. LA MINA DE LOS PROFUGOS

EN EL PRINCIPIO, TODAS LAS MINAS DE SANTA EULALIA,
CHIHUAHUA, DABAN 1/64 ANUAL DE TODA SU PRODUCCION A LA
CATEDRAL DE CHIHUAHUA, POR MAS DE 100 AÑOS. ORIGINALMENTE
HABIAN DONADO MAS DE 1 1/2 MILLONES PARA LA CONSTRUCCION
DE LA MISION EN 1790. HOY EN DIA, LA IGLESIA AUN RECIBE 1/64 AL
AÑO DE LA PRODUCCION DE **UNA** DE LAS MINAS SOBREVIVIENTES. A
FINALES DE 1800, OCHO HOMBRES ESCAPARON DE UNA PRISION Y SE
FUERON **MAS ALLA** DE DONDE ESTABAN ESTAS MINAS, EN LAS
COLINAS, LLENAS DE MINERALES, Y ENCONTRARON **OTRA** MINA.
MEXICO OFRECIO RECOMPENSA A LOS INDIOS PARA QUE LOS
ENCONTRARAN, PERO SIN RESULTADO ALGUNO. 15 AÑOS DESPUES
VINO A LA MISION UN INDIO QUE REPRESENTABA A LOS PROFUGOS,
PARA HABLAR CON EL PADRE. "ESTOS HOMBRES REQUERIAN EL
PERDON DE LA IGLESIA Y DE ESPAÑA, Y A CAMBIO OFRECIAN AL
GOBIERNO Y AL PADRE, **A AMBOS,** MAS DE UN MILLON EN PLATA."
EN MENOS DE SEIS MESES, EL CONVENIO FUE HECHO Y FIRMADO.
LOS PROFUGOS YA PERDONADOS VIVIERON MUY BIEN POR ALGUN
TIEMPO. TIEMPO DESPUES UNO DE LOS PROFUGOS REGRESO A SU
VIEJA MINA, Y EN SILENCIO ROBO MUCHAS DE LAS BARRAS DE
PLATA QUE HABIAN ESCONDIDO. TIEMPO DESPUES, HUBO UN
ATAQUE INDIO Y MATARON A LOS OCHOS HOMBRES Y A OTROS MAS.
EN LA ACTUALIDAD POCO SE SABE DE ESA MINA, EXCEPTO UNA IDEA
GENERAL DE DONDE ESTA. Y DE LAS BARRAS DE PLATA QUE AUN
ESPERAN SER DESCUBIERTAS. SE REQUIERE DE MUCHA
INVESTIGACION PARA ENCONTRAR ESTA MINA. YO EMPEZARIA CON
UNA VISITA A LA CATEDRAL, HABLA CON EL PADRE, CHECA LOS
ARCHIVOS ENTRE 1877 Y 1883 Y POR SUPUESTO, ORA.

9. EL TESORO DE PANCHO VILLA

DICEN QUE EL TESORO DE PANCHO VILLA ESTA ESCONDIDO EN
CALIFORNIA, ARIZONA, TEXAS Y MEXICO, Y QUE ALGO DEBE DE
ESTAR ESCONDIDO EN ALGUNO DE ESOS LUGARES. PERO LA MAYOR
PARTE DE SU TESORO, MONEDAS DE ORO, LINGOTES DE ORO Y
PLATA Y JOYAS, ESTAN ESCONDIDOS EN EL ESTADO DE DURANGO,
MEXICO.
EL PRESIDENTE DE LA HUERTA NO PUDO SACAR A PANCHO VILLA DE
DURANGO, ASI QUE LE ENTREGO TODO EL ESTADO PARA QUE LO
GOBERNARA A CAMBIO DE UN PAGO ANUAL DE 4 A 5 MILLONES DE
PESOS. EL TESORO DE PANCHO FUE TRAIDO DE DIFERENTES
LUGARES A LA PARTE NORTE DE MEXICO Y FUE ESCONDIDO EN LA
SIERRA MADRE DE SONORA. EL SIGUIENTE PRESIDENTE DE MEXICO,
ALVARO OBREGON, MANDO MATAR A PANCHO VILLA. UNO DE LOS
GENERALES QUE TRABAJABA CON PANCHO VILLA, ANTES DE
HABERSE ESCAPADO AL PASO, TEXAS, CUANDO ESCUCHO QUE
PANCHO VILLA HABIA SIDO MUERTO EN 1923, DICE; EL PROBLEMA
ES QUE PANCHO VILLA TENIA 4 O 5 HACIENDAS EN SONORA Y EL
ESCONDIO 3/4 PARTES DE SU TESORO A 500 VARAS DE UNA DE SUS
HACIENDAS, DENTRO DE UNA CUEVA. Y EL RESTO DE SU TESORO
FUE ENTERRADO BAJO UN ARBOL EN EL CENTRO DE UN CORRAL
ADYACENTE A OTRA DE SUS HACIENDAS. UNA DE LAS HACIENDAS
DE PANCHO VILLA ESTABA EN CANUTILLO, CHIHUAHUA. Y LA OTRA
EN CHIHUAHUA, CHIHUAHUA.

10. EL TESORO DE LA VILLA AZTECA

LOS ESPAÑOLES ESCUCHARON ACERCA DE GRANDES TESOROS,
COMO ORO, PLATA Y JADE QUE POSEIAN LOS AZTECAS EN SU VILLA,
LA INTENDENCIA DE SONORA, EN SINALOA. LOS ESPAÑOLES
CONTRATARON AL NEGRO ESTEBAN PARA QUE LOS LLEVARA HASTA
LA VILLA. LOS AZTECAS PELEARON FIRMEMENTE, PERO FUERON
DERROTADOS. ALGUNOS DE LOS AZTECAS ESCAPARON LLEVANDO
CONSIGO A ESTEBAN Y A ALGUNOS OTROS COMO PRISIONEROS. LOS
POCOS AZTECAS QUE QUEDARON VIVOS LES DIJERON QUE HABIAN
ESCUCHADO QUE LOS ESPAÑOLES VENIAN, ASI ES QUE ESCONDIERON
TODOS SUS TESOROS EN UNA GRAN CUEVA A DIA Y MEDIO DE

DISTANCIA, CAMINANDO(15-16 MILLAS) DE LA VILLA. LA CUEVA ESTA LOCALIZADA A LA ORILLA DEL VALLE QUE SON SEIS LEGUAS DE LARGO (12 1/2 - 13 MILES).

11. EL CANAL AL TESORO DE 3 1/4 DE LEGUA

LOS INDIOS YAQUI LE REVELARON A LOS ESPAÑOLES UNA FABULOSA MINA LLENA DE ORO QUE SE ENCUENTRA MUY CERCA DE LA MONTAÑA VACATETE, AL SURESTE DE MATEHUALA Y A 4 LEGUAS (8.6 MILLAS) AL ESTE DEL CERRO AZUL. EL ARRASTRE NO TENIA AGUA, ASI ES QUE TUVIERON QUE CABAR 3 1/4 LEGUAS (7 MILLAS) PARA PODER TRAER AGUA AL ARRASTRE QUE UNIA A UN PEQUEÑO LAGO QUE A SU VEZ UNIA LOS CAMPAMENTOS DE LOS MINEROS. EL CANAL LLEGO HASTA EL UNICO EDIFICIO PERMANENTE, LA IGLESIA DE ADOBE. LOS INDIOS SE REVELARON CONTRA LOS ESPAÑOLES Y VOLARON LA ENTRADA A LA MINA CON LOS CIENTOS DE BARRAS DE ORO QUE HABIA DENTRO, Y ASI MISMO DESTRUYERON EL CAMPAMENTO Y LA IGLESIA DE ADOBE QUE ALLI HABIA. LO QUE NO HICIERON FUE CERRAR EL CANAL DE 7 MILLAS QUE VENIA DESDE LAS MONTAÑAS. ENCUENTRA Y SIGUE EL CAÑON QUE TE LLEVA AL LAGO, SIGUE EL SENDERO MARCADO Y LOS MONUMENTOS HASTA LLEGAR A LA MINA.

12. 50 AÑOS DE TESORO

LA IGLESIA DE NUESTRA SEÑORA DE GUADALUPE, EN CIUDAD JUAREZ, FRENTE A LA CIUDAD DEL PASO, TENIA A UN INDIO CONVERTIDO COMO SU BENEFACTOR. EL INDIO LE TRIA AL PADRE DE LA IGLESIA ORO Y PLATA DE CUATRO A SEIS VECES AL AÑO. EL LE DIJO AL PADRE QUE DESDE SU MINA/CUEVA PODIA VER SU IGLESIA, Y QUE UNO DE LOS "CUARTOS" ESTABA LLENO DE BOLSAS VIEJAS DE ORO. EL INDIO FALLECIO SIN DECIRLE AL PADRE EN DONDE SE ENCONTRABA LA MINA, NO SIN ANTES DECIRLE QUE EN LA MINA "HABIA SUFICIENTE ORO PARA DARLE DE COMER A SU IGLESIA DURANTE 50 AÑOS". LA CUEVA/TUNEL ESTABA ABIERTA Y EN UN PLANO MUY INCLINADO, VIENDO HACIA LA IGLESIA.

13. EL SENDERO DEL TESORO DEL DIABLO

AL ANTIGUO SENDERO DE SONORA, DE SONORA A YUMA, ARIZONA, SE LLAMA CAMINO DEL DIABLO Y ESTA MAS O MENOS A 115 LEGUAS (250 MILLAS). ESTE SENDERO ERA INCREIBLEMENTE TRANSITADO. CASI NO HABIA AGUA, SOLAMENTE EN YUMA O EN EL MANANTIAL DE CARRIZO A 100 MILLAS A LO LARGO DEL SENDERO. Y DE LAS TINAJAS ALTAS A SONDITA, A 150 MILLAS, SOLO HABIA "TINAJAS" (TANQUES DE AGUA SOBRE LA MONTAÑA). HOY EN DIA, A LO LARGO DE ESTE SENDERO SE PUEDEN ENCONTRAR UNA VARIEDAD DE TESOROS Y ARTEFACTOS MUY GRANDES, EN FORMA DE COFRES, ARMAS, RUEDAS DE CARRETA Y OTRAS COSAS QUE FUERON ENTERRADAS PARA FACILITAR LA CARGA CUANDO LOS CABALLOS O LAS MULAS MORIAN, CON LA IDEA DE ALGUN DIA REGRESAR POR ELLAS. MONEDAS DE ORO Y JOYERO HAN SIDO ENCONTRADOS CERCA DE ESTE SENDERO. LLEVA AGUA Y UN DETECTOR DE METALES, Y MUCHA MAS AGUA, Y UNA CAMIONETA GRANDE, PARA PODER TRAER TODOS TUS TESOROS DE REGRESO. RECUERDA QUE LOS ARTEFACTOS TAMBIEN **SON** TESOROS, Y MUCHAS VECES DE MAYOR VALOR QUE EL ORO. ESTE SENDERO ES UN PARAISO PARA LA BUSCADORES DE MONEDAS. (VER EL MAPA DEL SENDERO EN LA PAGINA 2).

14. MONEDAS Y LINGOTES DE ORO

CERCA DEL PUEBLO LOS ALAMOS, EN EL RANCHO SANTA BARBARA, EN LA BASE DE LA MONTAÑA GUADALUPE, EN SONORA, HAY UN GRAN TESORO ESCONDIDO, UNA MINA DE LINGOTES DE ORO Y PLATA MUY FINA QUE AUN NO HA SIDO ENCONTRADA. LA HACIENDA DE DON FELIPE SE ENCONTRABA AL LADO DEL RIO MAYO, EL CUAL CONTINUA A TRAVES DEL VALLE MAYO Y HACIA EL MAR. TRES VECES POR SEMANA, UNA MANADA DE CABALLOS LLEVABA DE LA HACIENDA (ORO) Y MINAS (PLATA) DE DON FELIPE AL RANCHO SANTA BARBARA LINGOTES DE ORO Y PLATA FUNDIDOS. SUS MINAS DE PLATA ESTABAN EN LAS MONTAÑAS DE GUADALUPE Y SUS MINAS DE ORO AL OESTE DE SOBIA. DON FELIPE, FUE ASESINADO EN 1811 Y SU FAMILIA SE MUDO A LA CIUDAD DE MEXICO. SUS MINAS DE ORO

EN SOBIA NUNCA HAN SIDO ENCONTRADAS, Y AÑOS DESPUES, SU
HIJA "CLOTILDE" LE DIO A SU HIJO UN MAPA IMPERFECTO,
CONSTANDO QUE SU ABUELO HABIA ESCONDIDO MUCHOS LINGOTES
Y MONEDAS DE ORO PARA EMERGENCIAS, Y PARA LA COMPRA DE
GANADO BAJO UN GRAN ARBOL A 250 VARAS DE SU HACIENDA,
DIRECTAMENTE AFUERA DE LA VENTANA DE LA RECAMARA DE SU
PADRE. AMBOS, EL TESORO Y LAS MINAS, AUN NO HAN SIDO
ENCONTRADOS. A SU NIETO NUNCA LE HIZO FALTA EL DINERO, ASI
QUE NUNCA FUE EN BUSCA DEL TESORO O LA MINA ESCONDIDOS.
EL MAPA Y LA CARTA DE DON FELIPE RESURGIERON POR EL AÑO
1900, EN MANOS DE UN BUSCADOR DE TESOROS, PERO NUNCA PUDO
ENCONTRAR LA HACIENDA DE DON FELIPE....¿ Y TU ?

15. ARMADURAS, IDOLOS Y LA CAVERNA DEL TESORO DE LOS AZTECAS

ADYACENTE AL RIO DE SANTA CLARA, AL OESTE DE SAN JOSE DE LA
CRUZ, HAY UNA CUEVA CON LA ENTRADA MUY ANGOSTA QUE VA
HACIA LO PROFUNDO DE LA MONTAÑA Y SE CONVIERTE EN UNA
GRAN HABITACION LLENA DE LINGOTES O BARRAS DE ORO Y PLATA,
VIEJAS ARMADURAS Y BAULES LLENOS DE JOYAS Y ARTEFACTOS DE
ORO, Y DOS GRANDES IDOLOS DE ORO (18 PULGADAS). UN VIEJO
HOMBRE MEXICANO ENCONTRO ESTE TESORO POR ACCIDENTE Y LE
FUE POSIBLE VERLO GRACIAS A UN PEQUEÑO FUEGO QUE PRENDIO
EN LA CUEVA, PUES ESTA TENIA 3 O 4 SALIDAS DE AIRE/HUMO EN EL
TECHO. SE LLEVO ALGUNAS COSAS Y AL PARTIR, CERRO LA
ENTRADA Y LA MARCO CON TRES MADEROS MUERTOS. DESPUES
FUE A BUSCAR AL DIRECTOR DEL MUSEO NACIONAL DE MEXICO, Y
LE DIJO QUE POR UNA PEQUEÑA RECOMPENSA LE ENSEÑARIA EL
LUGAR DE LA MINA. EL DIRECTOR LE DIJO QUE LOS ARTEFACTOS
ERAN DE ORIGEN AZTECA PERO QUE SI HABIA ARMADURAS EN LA
CAVERNA PROBABLEMENTE FUERON ESCONDIDAS POR LOS
CONQUISTADORES. LA ESPOSA DEL DIRECTOR ESTABA MUY
ENFERMA, ASI QUE LE PIDIO AL HOMBRE QUE LE DIERA DOS
SEMANAS, Y ASIMISMO ESTE LE DIO TIEMPO AL DIRECTOR PARA
FORMAR UNA EXPEDICION HACIA EL LUGAR EN EL NOROESTE. EL
VIEJO HOMBRE SUFRIO UN ATAQUE, ASI QUE NO VIVIO EL TIEMPO

SUFICIENTE PARA LLEVAR AL GRUPO, DE MODO QUE EN 1956 EL
DIRECTOR ORGANIZO EL GRUPO DE OFICIALES Y ALGUNOS
SOLDADOS PARA BUSCAR LA CUEVA EN LA LOMA DE SANTA CLARA.
PASARON DOS SEMANAS PERO NO TENIAN NI EQUIPO NI DETECTOR
DE METALES QUE LES PUDIERA AYUDAR A ENCONTRARLO. CON EL
EQUIPO DE HOY EN DIA SERIA MAS FACIL ENCONTRARLO, MUCHO
MAS FACIL QUE SACARSE LA LOTERIA. LA UNICA OTRA CLAVE QUE
DEJO EL ANCIANO MEXICANO FUE; "DIRECTAMENTE BAJO LA
ENTRADA DE LA LOMA, A UNAS 200 VARAS DEL RIACHUELO DEL
CAÑON, AL EXPANDERSE POR AMBOS LADOS COMO UNA GRAN
ALBERCA, CON UN PEQUEÑO ISLOTE CERCA DEL CENTRO, DE MAS O
MENOS DIEZ VARAS CUADRADAS". - CUANDO LO ENCUENTRES,
MANDAME UNO DE LOS IDOLOS, PUES ME ENCANTAN.

16 EL TESORO MESA

EN EL NORTE DE SONORA HAY UN GRAN TESORO ESCONDIDO DE
ORO, PLATA Y JOYAS, AL ESTE DE CANAÑEA, CERCA DEL BORDE Y DE
LAS MONTAÑAS AJO. EL TESORO FUE DEJADO EN UNA CUEVA EN EL
LADO ESTE DE UNA PEQUEÑA **PLANICIE ALTA,** COMO A 65 MILLAS
DEL SURESTE DE NOGALES, MEXICO.

17 LOS TESOROS DE LA MISION PERDIDA

LA MISION PERDIDA DE SANTA ISABEL FUE CONSTRUIDA LEJOS DE
CUALQUIER ACTIVIDAD MINERA Y LEJOS DE LA POBLACION. ESTA
MISION SE ENCUENTRA A TRES DIAS CAMINANDO, AL ESTE DE SAN
AGUSTIN (APOXIMADAMENTE A 96 MILLAS). TRES MINEROS MUY
RICOS UNIERON FUERZAS PARA CONSTRUIR ESTA PEQUEÑA MISION
EN UN LUGAR TAN AISLADO DE TODO, PARA PODER OCULTAR SUS
TESOROS DEL GOBIERNO Y NO PAGAR IMPUESTOS, ETC. CADA UNO
DE LOS MINEROS CAVO UNA GRAN CUEVA PARA ESCONDER SU
TESORO, Y CONSIGUIERON A UN PADRE PARA QUE SE ENCARGARA
DE LA CONSTRUCCION DE ESTA MISION, Y PARA QUE NO HUBIERA
SOSPECHAS DE LOS MATERIALES TRANSPORTADOS ALLI, Y PARA
PODER LLEVARLOS DESPUES A SUS RESPECTIVAS CUEVAS. LA
MISION SE ENCUENTRA EN LA BASE DE UN DESPEÑADERO SOBRE

UNA PROLONGADA ELEVACION DE UN ANGOSTO CAÑON, CON UN
MANANTIAL QUE ALIMENTA AL LAGO. EL LAGO SE ENCUENTRA
RODEADO DE PLANTAS DE TABACO Y SEMILLAS DE FLECHA. EL PICO
DE SAN JUAN DE DIOS SE PODIA VER DESDE ESTA MISION. NUNCA SE
ENCONTRO LA ELEVADA PROLONGACION.

18 LA MONTAÑA DE LOS FRIJOLES DE ORO

EL PEQUEÑO PUEBLO DE CAMOA, EN EL RIO MAYO DE SONORA,
TENIA UN MISION, QUE ERA LA QUE SE BENEFICIABA DE LAS MINAS
MAS CERCANAS, LAS CUALES PRODUCIAN PEPITAS DE ORO DEL
TAMAÑO DE UN FRIJOL . LOS INDIOS MAYO LE ENSEÑARON AL
PADRE EL LUGAR DE LOS FRIJOLES DE ORO, Y EL PADRE A SU VEZ
CONSTRUYO UN TUNEL HACIA LA MINA QUE UTILIZABA CUANDO
HACIA FALTA DINERO. LA MINA SE TRABAJABA DOS MESES AL AÑO
O CADA DOS AÑOS, Y DURANTE EL RESTO DEL TIEMPO, EL PADRE
MANTENIA LA ENTRADA A LA MINA CERRADA. EN EL PUEBLO DE
CAMOA LOS INDIOS SE SUBLEVARON, Y POCO TIEMPO DESPUES EL
PADRE FUE ARRESTADO Y SACADO DE MEXICO. CAMOA SE
MANTUVO INHABITABLE HASTA EL AÑO DE 1850, Y DURANTE LA
RECONSTRUCCION DEL PUEBLO, SE CAVO DEBAJO DE LA HACIENDA
Y SE ENCONTRO UN COFRE CON UNA CORONA DE ORO, UNA DAGA
DE ORO Y UN ANTIGUO DOCUMENTO QUE ESTABA MANCHADO Y
PODRIDO. DE CUALQUIER MANERA, LO QUE SE PODIA LEER DECIA,
"ESTOY PARADO EN LA PUERTA PRINCIPAL DEL RELICARIO Y MIRO
HACIA EL **SURESTE** A LA GRAN MONTAÑA, Y VEO EL ARRECIFE DE
PIEDRAS QUE SUJETA EL TUNEL QUE ARROJA LOS FRIJOLES DE ORO
EN GRANDES CANTIDADES." CERCA DE ALLI HAY UNA MONTAÑA
QUE LOS INDIOS SOLIAN LLAMAR " MANI DE ORO", PERO MUCHOS
CREEN QUE ESTA NO ES LA MONTAÑA. BUSCA EL ARRECIFE DE
PIEDRAS PROMINENTES.

19 TIBURON, LA ISLA DE TESOROS

LAS AGUAS QUE RODEAN LA ISLA TIBURON SON EL HOGAR DE
MUCHOS FEROCES TIBURONES, SIN EMBARGO, LOS INDIOS SERI,
QUIENES VIVIAN EN ESTA ISLA POR EL AÑO DE 1900, ERAN AUN MAS

FEROCES QUE ESTOS TIBURONES. LOS INDIOS SERI ERAN CANIBALES, Y ADEMAS ERAN MUY POSESIVOS CON SU ISLA Y MATABAN A TODOS LOS INTRUSOS CON DARDOS, FLECHAS Y LANZAS PONZOÑOSAS EXTRAIDOS DE LAS MILES DE SERPIENTES QUE HABIA EN ESTA ISLA DE 14 POR 28 MILLAS DE LARGO, LA CUAL SE ENCUENTRA CERCA DE LA COSTA ESTE DEL GOLFO DE CALIFORNIA. EL INTERIOR ES ALTO Y ESCABROSO, CON POCOS MANANTIALES Y MUCHOS MATORRALES DE PALMA. LAS TROPAS FEDERALES DE MEXICO "INVADIERON" LA ISLA CUATRO VECES PARA PODER REESTABLECER A LOS INDIOS SERIS EN EL CONTINENTE Y ASI PODER "CONTROLARLOS". AL CUARTO INTENTO LO LOGRARON, Y AHORA LA VILLA DE LOS INDIOS SERI SE ENCUENTRA EN EL CONTINENTE, A 20 MILLAS DE UN FARO, Y DOS CUARTELES FEDERALES ESTAN EN LA ISLA. HA SIDO **DOCUMENTADO** QUE MUCHOS, PERO MUCHOS TESOROS, HAN SIDO ENTERRADOS EN LA ISLA TIBURON POR MUCHOS PIRATAS, BARCOS FRANCESES E INGLESES, ASI COMO TAMBIEN SE DICE QUE LOS TESOROS DE LOS AZTECAS Y DE LOS INDIOS SERI ESTAN ENTERRADOS ALLI. CUERPOS DE METAL DE ORO FUERON LOCALIZADOS A MENOS DE 6 PIES BAJO LA SUPERFICIE POR UN GEOLOGO-EXPLORADOR INGLES. EL TENIENTE C. ROVINSON DE INGLATERRA Y OTROS EN SU GRUPO FUERON ASESINADOS EN LA PLAYA MIENTRAS CARGABAN PARTE DE LOS TESOROS RECOBRADOS. EL CAPITAN G. PORTER, DEL BARCO AMERICANO "WORLD", Y DOS MIEMBROS DE SU TRIPULACION FUERON CLAVADOS A TRES ARBOLES A LO LARGO DE LA PLAYA EN 1907. EL PROFESOR H. E. MILLER, SUPERINTENDENTE DE LAS ESCUELAS EN ARIZONA, FUE ASESINADO JUNTO CON EL CAPITAN GUS ORLANDER, DEL BARCO "ELIZA", MIENTRAS SE EMPEÑABAN EN LOCALIZAR UN PUNTO DEPOSITADO EN TIBURON. ESTO FUE MUCHO TIEMPO DESPUES DE QUE SE LES PROHIBIO A LOS INDIOS SERI REGRESAR A LA ISLA. ¿ ESTARAN LON INDIOS AUN CUIDANDO SU HOGAR CERCANO ? LA ISLA TIBURON ES DE FACIL ACCESO POR BARCO, Y UN DETECTOR DE METALES PROFUNDOS PODRIA TRANSFORMARTE EN UN "MULTIMILLONARIO" RAPIDAMENTE. NO ESTOY MUY SEGURO SI VALE LA PENA JUGARSELA.

20 EL TESORO AZTECA DE LA MESA DE LOS TOROS

DE TRES A CUATRO TONELADAS DE ORO, PLATA Y ORNAMENTOS,

FUERON ESCONDIDOS BAJO "LA MESA DE LOS TOROS" POR LOS AZTECAS, LUGAR QUE ESTA APROXIMADAMENTE A 14 LEGUAS CAMINANDO (30MILLAS), DE CHOIX, EN EL RIO CHOIX. FUE ORDENADO QUE TODOS LOS TESOROS DE LA VILLA FUERAN PUESTOS EN LA "CUEVA PINTADA", QUE ESTA LOCALIZADA, SEGUN LOS REPORTES, A MUY CORTA DISTANCIA DE LA ORILLA OESTE DEL ARROYO DEL TORO, EN EL RIACHUELO DEL CAÑON. EL JEFE DE LA VILLA AZTECA FUE ALERTADO DE LOS ESPAÑOLES QUE SE APROXIMABAN Y DIO LA SIGUIENTE ORDEN, DOCUMENTADA POR "ESTEVAN": ME PONDRE DE PIE MAÑANA POR LA MAÑANA, CON LA ESPALDA HACIA EL TORO, Y CUANDO MI SOMBRA SE PROYECTE SOBRE LA CUEVA PINTADA QUE ESTA DEL LADO OPUESTO DEL CAÑON, TODOS NUESTROS TESOROS ESTARAN DENTRO DE ESTA CUEVA, Y LA CUEVA SERA SELLADA. ESTA CUEVA DEL TESORO NUNCA HA SIDO ENCONTRADA; SIN EMBARGO, AUN HOY, DESPUES DE LAS INUNDACIONES FUERTES DEL ARROYO, PEQUEÑOS PEDAZOS DE ORO Y PLATA Y ORNAMENTOS SE ENCUENTRAN EN EL RIACHUELO.

21. PLAYAS DE ORO Y JOYAS

HAY MUCHAS AREAS DE PLAYAS EN MEXICO EN LAS QUE SE HAN DESCUBIERTO TESOROS ANUALMENTE DURANTE CIENTOS DE AÑOS, USUALMENTE POR GENTE CON DETECTORES DE METALES O TRAS TORMENTAS POR GENTE CON "OJOS DE AGUILA". ALGUNAS DE LAS "PLAYAS" SON DE SOLAMENTE UNOS CUANTOS PIES DE ANCHO DURANTE LA MAREA BAJA, Y SON DIFICILES DE DESCUBRIR, PERO AUN ASI VALE LA PENA EL ESFUERZO.
A TRAVES DE LAS COSTAS DEL **GOLFO DE MEXICO**, TANTO TESOROS ESPAÑOLES COMO AZTECAS SON DESCUBIERTOS POR LA MAREA, PROVENIENTES DE GALEONES ESPAÑOLES QUE NAUFRAGARON CERCA DE LA ORILLA, EN SU MAYOR PARTE DEBIDO A GRANDES TORMENTAS Y HURACANES. EN LA DECADA DE 1960, UN HOMBRE CAMINANDO CON LA RODILLA EN EL AGUA TOPO SU PIE CON UNA BARRA DE PLATA DE 62 LIBRAS. DURANTE LOS SIGUIENTES SEIS MESES ENCONTRO TESOROS POR MAS DE $300,000.00 DOLARES, AL ARRASTRAR SUS PIES ALREDEDOR DEL AREA DE MUY POCA

PROFUNDIDAD DE AGUA. LAS PLAYAS DEL **GOLFO DE MEXICO** SON LAS MAS RICAS.

A TRAVES DEL **OCEANO PACIFICO** Y EN LA PARTE ALTA DE EL **MAR DE CORTES/GOLFO DE CALIFORNIA** TAMBIEN SE ENCUENTRAN TESOROS EN LAS PLAYAS. ESTOS PROVIENEN DE GALEONES NAUFRAGADOS DE MANILA Y BARCOS PIRATAS, AUNQUE ALGUNOS TESOROS POSIBLEMENTE FUERON ENTERRADOS, Y DESPUES DESCUBIERTOS POR LAS TORMENTAS. EN SU MAYOR PARTE DOBLONES DE ORO EN PIEZAS DE OCHO Y ANILLOS, SON ENCONTRADOS EN ESTOS LUGARES DE LA **BAJA CALIFORNIA**.

22. CUEVAS DE TESOROS ESPAÑOLES/AZTECAS

EN 1948, UN GRAN TESORO AZTECA FUE ENCONTRADO ALREDEDOR DE 90 MILLAS AEREAS AL NORESTE DE LA CIUDAD DE MEXICO, EN LAS MONTAÑAS, 8 MILLAS AL SUR DEL PEQUEÑO PUEBLO DE "TETELA". MANUEL RAMIREZ HA PASADO LA MAYOR PARTE DE SU VIDA BUSCANDO ESTE TESORO Y OTRAS DOS CUEVAS CON TESOROS ESCONDIDAS EN LOS ALREDEDORES. MANUEL HA DADO TRES MAPAS DE SU SUEGRO EN AÑOS ANTERIORES, QUIEN LE DIJO QUE TRES CUEVAS, TODAS DENTRO DEL PERIMETRO DE UNA MILLA ENTRE ELLAS, ESTABAN LLENAS DE TESOROS ESCONDIDOS POR BANDIDOS QUE ROBARON UNA CARAVANA, LA CUAL LLEVABA EL TESORO HACIA VERACRUZ PARA SER EMBARCADO A ESPAÑA. EN 1948, MANUEL Y SUS CUATRO HIJOS ENCONTRARON Y ABRIERON UNA DE LAS CUEVAS - SE CORRIO LA VOZ Y EL GOBIERNO MEXICANO INTERVINO Y LO EMBARGO TODO. EN LOS PERIODICOS DE LA CIUDAD DE MEXICO SE PODIA LEER ACERCA DEL "GRAN TESORO AZTECA ENCONTRADO" CERCA DE "TETELA" - Y ENTONCES - NO MAS HISTORIAS NI INFORMACION. PARECE SER QUE EL GOBIERNO NO QUERIA HABLAR DE ELLO. - O REVELAR QUE ES LO QUE HICIERON CON EL TESORO. CERCA DE DOS AÑOS MAS TARDE, MANUEL FUE ENTREVISTADO (EL Y SUS 4 HIJOS HABIAN PERMANECIDO EN LA CARCEL DURANTE 6 MESES), Y EL DIJO QUE SUS OTROS DOS MAPAS DE LAS OTRAS CUEVAS DE TESOROS ESTABAN PERDIDOS - PERO QUE

NO IMPORTABA YA QUE SABIA QUE ERAN TESOROS "NACIONALES", Y QUE ERA ILEGAL PARA "INDIVIDUOS POSEER TALES TESOROS NACIONALES". MUCHAS DE LAS LEYES MEXICANAS HAN CAMBIADO DESDE 1948 - QUIZA NO HAYA PROBLEMA EN ENCONTRAR UN TESORO AZTECA HOY EN DIA. SI ASI ES, YO BUSCARIA CON SEGURIDAD EN UN RADIO DE 1 MILLA ALREDEDOR DE LA CUEVA QUE MANUEL Y SUS HIJOS ENCONTRARON.

23. LA CAVERNA DEL CRANEO Y DEL TESORO

CERCA DE 6 MILLAS AL SUR, SUROESTE DE "COBA", EN LA JUNGLA, HAY UN AREA SEMIPANTANOSA DE 20 A 30 ACRES DE TAMAÑO, Y EN LA ORILLA OESTE DE ESTA ZONA BAJA SE LEVANTA UNA ROCA PROMINENTE DE CERCA DE 15 PIES DE ALTURA, 60 PIES DE LARGO Y 30 PIES DE ANCHO **QUE PARECE UNA GRAN HOGAZA DE PAN**. MARTIN G. FARNSWORTH, UN ESTUDIANTE ACAUDALADO (A LA EDAD DE 46 AÑOS) DE ARQUEOLOGIA DE INGLATERRA, ESCRIBIO LO SIGUIENTE EN SU DIARIO BIENAL , ENFATIZANDO SUS ACTIVIDADES EN YUCATAN Y ALREDEDORES. MARTIN MURIO EN LA JUNGLA YUCATECA DE ALGUN TIPO DE ENVENENAMIENTO ACCIDENTAL, DE ACUERDO CON LOS REPORTES DE LOS GUIAS NATIVOS Y TRABAJADORES.

LAS NOTAS DE MARTIN REVELAN UNA FASCINACION POR ESTA ROCA EN FORMA DE HOGAZA DE PAN - PARECIA HECHA POR EL HOMBRE PERO NO LO ERA. UNOS 8 MESES ANTES DE MORIR, SU DIARIO DECLARA: "AL PASAR POR LA HOGAZA DE PAN HOY NOTE LA PUNTA DE UNA POSIBLE ENTRADA DE CUEVA/TUNEL, A NIVEL DE AGUA DEL PANTANO. ENFATICE ESTO, POR LO QUE LA LIMPIAREMOS E INDAGAREMOS EN LA PRIMERA OPORTUNIDAD. DOS SEMANAS MAS TARDE, CON LA AYUDA DE TRONCOS Y PALOS ENCONTRAMOS Y ENTRAMOS EN UN TUNEL QUE SE ABRIA DENTRO DE LA CAVERNA MAYOR, CON ESCALONES ESCULPIDOS QUE LLEVABAN ARRIBA DEL NIVEL DE TIERRA HACIA UN CUARTO CON NICHOS DE 11" DE ANCHO POR 14" DE ALTO, CORTADOS DENTRO DE LAS PAREDES, CADA UNO CON UN CRANEO FRENTE A MI (QUIZA 250). ALGO DE LUZ ENTRA A TRAVES DE LOS 47 HOYOS DEL DOMO DE ESTA ROCA - CADA UNO CON DIAMETRO DE 4" A 8". HACIA LA PARTE FINAL HAY UNA PARED

PLANA DE CERCA DE 10 PIES DE ALTO POR 20 PIES DE ANCHO, CON DISEÑOS DE COLORES Y PETROGLIFICOS. EL SUELO PLANO QUE SE EXTIENDE BAJO LAS MARCAS ESTA LLENO DE JARRONES, TAZONES, OBJETOS DE ORO, TURQUESA, CUCHILLOS Y OBJETOS DE PLATA. TOME 34 FOTOS. ME QUEDE CON EL PEQUÑO ANIMAL DE ORO Y EL CUCHILLO DE MANGO DE ORO Y JADE MOSTRADOS AL FRENTE DE MIS FOTOS.

MIS HOMBRES ESTAN MUY DISGUSTADOS Y NO SE ATREVEN A TOCAR NADA YA QUE PIENSAN QUE TODO ESTA "PROTEGIDO" POR LOS CRANEOS (ESPIRITUS). MOVIMOS NUESTRA PARED DE TRONCOS Y PALOS - NO ME LLEVARE MAS OBJETOS POR EL MOMENTO".
SEIS DIAS DEPUES EN SU DUARIO - LA FOTO DE LA HABITACION, LA MANDE A CASA (INGLATERRA) PARA QUE FRUERA REVELADA. LOS GRANDES DESCUBRIMIENTOS DE MARTIN EN SU DIARIO NUNCA MAS FUERON MENCIONADOS. LAS FOTOS NUNCA LLEGARON A SU FAMILIA EN INGLATERRA, PERO SU DIARIO SI. AUN NO HA SIDO ENCONTRADO O AL MENOS SIN REPORTE.

24. EL PEQUEÑO TEMPLO MAYA

EN 1981, EL (GRUPO ARQUEOLOGICO MAYA) M.A.G., DE FLORIDA, GUIADO POR GENE HEARTMAN, LOCALIZO EL PEQUEÑO TEMPLO O ESTRUCTURA MAYA A UNAS CUANTAS MILLAS AL SUR DE YUCATAN, FRONTERA CON QUINTANA ROO, AL SUROESTE DEL PUERTO ARTURO. HEARTMAN REPORTO A LAS AUTORIDADES DE SUS HALLAZGOS, Y PIDIO GUARDIAS Y OFICIALES PARA QUE PROTEGIERAN ESTE PROYECTO A SU REGRESO. DIJO QUE IBA A LA FLORIDA Y A CALIFORNIA A CONSEGUIR UN GRUPO PARA FILMAR Y DOCUMENTAR SUS HALLAZGOS.
DESAFORTUNADAMENTE, A HEARTMAN SE LE ENCONTRO PASANDO DE CONTRABANDO A LOS ESTADOS UNIDOS UN HACHA DE ORO, SEIS DISCOS DE ORO DE 3 1/2" POR 4 1/4", TRES BROCHES EN FORMA/DISEÑO DE VIBORAS Y UN OBJETO DE ORO SOLIDO CON INSCRIPCIONES Y DISEÑOS DE 8 1/4" POR 11 1/3" POR 1/2". DE ALGUNA MANERA "COMPRO" SU SALIDA DE MEXICO Y ES "UNA PERSONA NO GRATA" - Y SU FABULOSO PEQUEÑO TEMPLO AUN NO HA SIDO ENCONTRADO.

25. RIO SUBTERRANEO CON IDOLOS DE ORO

COMO A 90 MILLAS AL ESTE DE ACAPULCO Y 30 MILLAS AL NORTE
ALREDEDOR DEL PUNTO MEDIO ENTRE QUETZALAPA Y
IXCUINATOYAC, SE ENCUENTRA EN UNA MONTAÑA AL FINAL DE
UNA ELEVACION PROLONGADA QUE SE PRECIPITA HACIA UN VALLE,
HACIA UNA AREA BAJA DEL DESIERTO. ALLI, EN EL PUNTO DE
PRECIPITADO, SE ENCUENTRA UNA GRAN ABERTURA UN POCO
IRREGULAR, DE TAL MANERA QUE SE EXTIENDE HACIA ABAJO AL
NIVEL DEL DESIERTO.

ESTA ES MAS O MENOS EL AREA EN DONDE RAMON CUIDABA LAS
OVEJAS Y VACAS DE SU FAMILIA. UN DIA, RAMON VIO LA ABERTURA
Y LE DIJO A SU PAPA Y HERMANOS. - "TAL VEZ SEA UNA VIEJA MINA
ESPAÑOLA Y MUY RICA". EL PADRE SUPERVISABA, MIENTRAS SUS
HIJOS BAJABAN CON LINTERNAS Y ANTORCHAS. LA CUEVA
CONTINUABA BAJANDO, Y EN EL CAMINO ENCONTRARON "MESAS"
CON CHIMINEAS Y OLLAS CON HUESOS. LES TOMO MAS DE UN AÑO Y
CERCA DE DIEZ VIAJES LLEGAR HASTA EL FONDO (UNAS CUATRO
HORAS HASTA EL FONDO DE LA CUEVA), EN DONDE ENCONTRARON
UN PEQUEÑO Y TRANQUILO RIO PROFUNDO DE 25' A 30' DE ANCHO
CON UN GRAN AREA AL OTRO LADO DEL RIO. LANZARON UNA
ANTORCHA HACIA EL OTRO LADO Y LES PARECIO VER UNOS
OBJETOS EN EL SUELO. SOLO JESUS SABIA NADAR, Y NO QUERIA
CRUZAR. SU PADRE LO CONVENCIO DE QUE CRUZARA NADANDO
PARA VER QUE HABIA DEL OTRO LADO. EL PAPA TRAJO GRANDES
LINTERNAS QUE PARECIAN ILUMINAR **OBJETOS DE ORO** DEL OTRO
LADO DEL ANGOSTO RIO.

RAMON Y SUS HERMANOS SACARON UN TORO DE ORO DE NUEVE
LIBRAS Y DOS TAZAS DE ORO DE DOS LIBRAS, Y REPORTARON QUE
HABIA DE 100 A 120 OBJETOS DE ORO COMO DE 4" A 10" DE ALTO,
IGUALMENTE SEPARADOS UNO DE OTRO COMO POR UNA VARA, Y
QUE ESTABAN POR TODOS EL SUELO.

RAMON Y SUS HERMANOS PLANEARON UN VIAJE DE 10 DIAS PARA
SACAR LOS DEMAS OBJETOS. NUNCA REGRESARON DEL VIAJE. LA
ESPOSA DE RAMON Y MADRE DE SU HIJOS CONTO SU HISTORIA A UN
AMIGO, PARA QUE FUERA A BUSCARLOS, Y LE DIO UNA DE LAS
TAZAS DE ORO, PERO NI LA ENTRADA NI SU EQUIPO FUERON
ENCONTRADOS. COMO UN AÑO DESPUES, ELLA FUE A SAN MARCOS

CON SU PRIMO A VER AL JEFE DE POLICIA. LE MOSTRO EL TORO DE
ORO Y LE DIO A LA OTRA TAZA DE ORO, Y LE DIJO: "YO SE QUE YA
ESTAN CON DIOS. HAY QUE ENTERRARLOS Y BENDECIRLOS
PROPIAMENTE". "ESTA TAZA DE ORO ES PARA TI, Y ESTE TORO SERA
TU RECOMPENSA CUANDO LOS ENCUENTRES, MAS TODO EL
TESORO". EL JEFE DE LA POLICIA CONTRATO HOMBRES PARA
BUSCARLOS, Y HASTA EL MISMO FUE A BUSCARLOS HASTA EL DIA EN
QUE MURIO, EN 1986 - Y AUN NO LOS ENCUENTRAN.

26. ASI QUE, ¿5 MILLONES?

AL PIE DE UNA PEQUEÑA EXTENSION DE MONTAÑAS, COMO A 20
MILLAS DE "MONCLOVA", ESTA EL PEQUEÑO PUEBLO "LAS CABRAS".
HACE MUCHOS AÑOS HABIA UNA PEQUEÑA HACIENDA ESPAÑOLA AL
PIE DE ESTAS MONTAÑAS, Y SU DUEÑO ERA DON ALFONSO DE
MADRID. EL PRESIDENTE DE MEXICO LE ORDENO/PIDIO A DON
ALFONSO QUE REGRESARA A ESPAÑA EN 1928,Y ESTE SE FUE
RAPIDAMENTE. CINCO AÑOS MAS TARDE, DON ALFONSO LE ESCRIBIO
LA SIGUIENTE CARTA AL PADRE DE LA CATEDRAL DE MONCLOVA.
ESTA CARTA REAPARECIO EN LOS ARCHIVOS DE LA CATEDRAL A
MEDIADOS DE 1980.

JUNIO 6 DE 1833.

QUERIDO PADRE ENRNESTO:

HAN PASADO MUCHOS AÑOS Y RUEGO A DIOS QUE USTED SE
ENCUENTRE BIEN - ETC.
NI MI ESPOSA NI YO ESTAREMOS DE REGRESO COMO ESPERABAMOS
Y ORAMOS. ASI QUE LE DOY A LA IGLESIA Y A USTED LA MITAD DE
MIS POSESIONES EN LA HACIENDA. LA OTRA MITAD LE PIDO QUE LAS
DEJE ALLI EN CASO DE QUE MI ESPOSA O YO REGRESEMOS.
"USTED RECORDARA QUE EL DIA QUE BAUTIZO A MI HIJO MIGUEL
ESTABAMOS PARADOS JUNTO A AL POZO EN MI HACIENDA, BAJO LA
SOMBRA DE AQUEL GRAN ARBOL. SEIS VARAS BAJO EL ANILLO, Y EN
EL LADO OESTE DE LA PARED, ES ALLI EN DONDE SE ESCONDE EL
PASADIZO DE MI CUARTO DE LOS 5 MILLONES EN ORO".

NO SABEMOS SI EL PADRE FUE POR SU MITAD - PERO LA OTRA MITAD
PUEDE QUE AUN ESTE ALLI. - ESPERANDO.   (VER LA PAGINA 13)

27. EL TESORO DE LAS ROCAS DEL REFUGIO

A FINES DE 1400 UTILIZABAN CODIGOS DE PIRATAS, SEÑALES,
SIMBOLOS Y MONUMENTOS PARA COMUNICARSE Y DEJARESE
MENSAJES PRIVADAMENTE ALREDEDOR DEL MUNDO. EL "TESORO
DEL REFUGIO", VISTO EN LA PAGINA 15, FUE UN MONUMENTO QUE
ELLOS CONSTRUYERON EN UNA **ISLA** O A LA **ENTRADA DE UN
PUERTO,** O A LO **LARGO DE UNA COSTA,** PARA DAR A ENTENDER UN
MENSAJE, "ESTA ES UN AREA **PROTEGIDA CONTRA EL CLIMA -
ANCLAS O MAS BARCOS**". BAJO LA LOMA DE "PUNTA MITA" AL
NORTE DEL FAMOSO PUERTO VALLARTA, ESTUVO UNO DE ESTOS,
DICIENDO A LOS BARCOS PIRATAS QUE ESTE ERA UN PUERTO
PROTEGIDO/**PROTEGIDO DEL CLIMA.**
A PRINCIPIOS DE 1600 LOS ESPAÑOLES CONOCIERON EL SIGNIFICADO
PIRATA DE ESTOS MONUMENTOS Y COMENZARON A USAR DICHOS
MONUMENTOS **TIERRA ADENTRO** MUY FRECUENTEMENTE.
**ENTIERRA/ESCONDE TESOROS BAJO ESTOS MONUMENTOS DE
PIEDRA.** UNA "GRAN ROCA DE REFUGIO DEL TESORO" FUE QUITADA
MIENTRAS NIVELABAN UN PUNTO EN LA COSTA CERCA DE MIAMI,
FLORIDA, PARA LA CONSTRUCCION DE UN GRAN HOTEL EN 1938.
LOS PERIODICOS REPORTARON UN HALLAZGO ESTIMADO EN 11
MILLONES DE DOLARES, ENTERRADOS EN EL CENTRO DE LA ROCA,
ESCONDIDOS PROBABLEMENTE POR LOS ESPAÑOLES. SIN EMBARGO,
ERA MAS LOGICO QUE LOS PIRATAS HUBIERAN ENTERRADO ESTE
TESORO.
MANTENTE ALERTA CON ESTOS MONUMENTOS ESCULTURAS/CORTES
DE REFUGIO EN DONDE SEA QUE LOS ENCUENTRES. LAS ENTRADAS A
MINAS Y/O TESOROS PUEDEN ESTAR **BAJO ESTA GRAN ROCA** QUE
ESTA ESCULPIDA DE TAL MANERA QUE NORMALMENTE DE 4 A 6
PERSONAS CABEN EN LA PARTE HUECA, Y SER PROTEGIDOS DE LA
LLUVIA.

28. TERRAPLENES DE ENTIERRO DE TESOROS

UN MUCHACHO COMO DE 16 AÑOS, INDIO NATIVO, DIJO A UN GRUPO DE ARQUELOLOGOS ALEMANES EN 1987 QUE CUANDO EL TENIA MAS O MENOS OCHO AÑOS, SE FUE CON SU PAPA A LA JUNGLA, UN POCO AL OESTE DE "BECANCHEN" (COMO A 90 MILLAS AL ESTE DE "CAMPECHE"), Y VIERON A UN PEQUEÑO VENADO EN UNA PROLONGACION ELEVADA COMO A 40 PIES ARRIBA DE ELLOS. EL VENADO SE MOVIA RAPIDAMENTE, PERO NO CORRIO, ASI QUE EL PADRE Y EL HIJO SUBIERON. "NOS DIMOS CUENTA DE QUE EL VENADO TENIA UNA DE SUS PATAS ATRAPADAS ENTRE LA TIERRA Y UNA GRAN ROCA PLANA COMO DE 600 A 800 LIBRAS QUE SE ENCONTRABA EN ESA PROLONGACION. MATAMOS AL VENADO Y SACAMOS SU PIE DE LA TIERRA. MI PADRE MIRO HACIA ABAJO Y METIO POR EL HOYO UN PALO LARGO. DESPUES CAVAMOS UN POQUITOY AVENTAMOS PIEDRAS QUE NOS MOSTRARON QUE ERA PROFUNDO Y DE SUELO DURO. REGRESAMOS CON CUERDAS, PALAS Y LINTERNAS Y CAVAMOS HASTA QUE NOS TOPAMOS CON ROCA, ASI QUE MOVIMOS UN POCO LA GRAN ROCA, LO SUFICIENTE PARA PODER METER MI CABEZA, UN BRAZO Y UNA LINTERNA PARA VER QUE HABIA EN EL FONDO. HABIA CUERPOS ACOSTADOS EN GRANDES ROCAS PLANAS, TAZONES Y MUCHOS OBJETOS SOBRE PEQUEÑAS ROCAS Y MUCHOS OBJETOS DE ORO - ESTOY SEGURO. NO TENIAMOS HERRAMIENTAS PARA ROMPER LA ROCA O AGRANDAR EL HOYO PARA QUE MI PADRE PUDIERA VER. ESA NOCHE TAPAMOS NUESTRO HOYO CON UNA PIEDRA Y TIERRA Y NOS FUIMOS A CASA. MI PADRE SE CAYO Y SE HIRIO LA PIERNA SERIAMENTE. DEJAMOS LA CARNE DEL VENADO Y LAS HERRAMIENTAS CERCA DE ALLI. NOS TOMO DOS DIAS REGRESAR A LA CASA, Y LA PIERNA DE MI PADRE ESTABA HINCHADA Y LLENA DE VENENO. DIEZ DIAS MAS TARDE MI PADRE MURIO. MI MAMA ME DIJO: 'NUNCA REGRESES ALLI, LOS ESPIRITUS MATARON A TU PADRE'. EL MUCHACHO LES DIJO A LOS ALEMANES "ESTOY SEGURO DE QUE YO LOS PUEDO LLEVAR ALLI, SI ME PAGAN" EL TRATO DE LLEVARLOS, PERO NO PUDO ENCONTRAR LA PARTE BAJA DE LA PROLONGACION ROCOSA CON LA GRAN ROCA PLANA QUE CUBRIA LA ENTRADA O EL HOYO DE HUMO CUBIERTO - AUN SIGUE SIN ENCONTRARSE.

"Treasure-Signs, Symbols, Shadows and Sun Signs"

©TX-3-225535
ISBN 0-932156-0-4

"Spanish Monuments & Trailmakers to Treasure"

©TX-577402
ISBN 0-9632156-1-2

"Death Traps to Treasure"

©TXu652-300
ISBN 0-9632156-2-0

"Unfound Treasures of Mexico"

(Español & English)
ISBN 0-9632156-4-7

El Proximo Libro

"Treasure Secrets of the Lost Dutchman"

ISBN 0-9632156-3-9